Finesse 'Em

How to Get What You Want Without a Sledgehammer

Finesse 'Em

HOW TO GET WHAT YOU WANT WITHOUT A SLEDGEHAMMER

BY

PETER DAVIDSON

CeShore

CeShore

ISBN 1-58501-013-8

Trade Paperback
© Copyright 2000 Peter Davidson
All rights reserved
First Printing—2000
Library of Congress #99-64522

Request for information should be addressed to:

CeShore Publishing Co.
The Sterling Building
440 Friday Road
Pittsburgh, PA 15209
www.ceshore.com

Cover Art: Michelle Vennare - SterlingHouse Publisher, Inc.
Typesetting: Tracy Lynn Reedy

CeShore is an imprint of SterlingHouse Publisher.

Printed in Canada

To Bev and Nancy for your interest, support,
encouragement and assistance—thanks.

CONTENTS

PREFACE

For a long time, now, I've been intrigued and fascinated by those people who can solve life's problems and remove obstacles from their path without breaking a sweat.

They don't yell, scream, holler, or use force, fear, or intimidation to get their way. Instead, they are clever and imaginative. They use tact, creativity, and strategy. In short, they use *finesse* instead of a sledgehammer.

For the past six years, I've gathered examples of how people, including myself, have solved seemingly difficult or impossible problems in unique and clever ways. And, I've observed how people have created tactical strategies to make their lives easier, less stressful, and more successful.

This book consists of over sixty-five true stories, scenarios, and essays in six categories that serve as examples of how to get what you want through creativity, tact, strategy, and finesse rather than through force, fear, and intimidation.

I hope you find these examples to be interesting, eye-opening, and even humorous, sometimes. But more than this, I hope you find them to be inspiring. Inspiring enough so that, when you are faced with life's problems and obstacles, you will choose to solve them through finesse, rather than with a sledgehammer.

Peter Davidson

To My Friends, Neighbors and Relatives

If you think you recognize yourself in one of these stories, it is you if you want it to be. If you don't, it isn't. It's somebody else. Relax, your story's safe with me.

Peter

I.
Developing Finesse

When it comes to creating solutions to problems and devising methods for removing obstacles from one's path, it seems almost everyone has an opinion or two. Here's some you might enjoy and learn from:

> *Force is all conquering, but its victories are short-lived.* Abraham Lincoln

> *The greatest conqueror is he who overcomes the enemy without a blow.* Chinese proverb

> *If the only tool you have is a hammer, you tend to see every problem as a nail.* Abraham Maslow

> *There is one thing stronger than all the armies in the world, that is an idea whose time has come.* Victor Hugo

> *The greatest truths are the simplest.* A.W. Hare

> *The ability to ask the right question is more than half the battle of finding the answer.* Thomas J. Watson

> *The secret of creativity is knowing how to hide your sources.* Albert Einstein

> *Nothing you can't spell will ever work.* Will Rogers

Depend on the rabbit's foot if you will, but remember it didn't work for the rabbit. R.E. Shay

Tact is the knack of making a point without making an enemy. Howard W. Newton

A diplomat is a person who can tell you to go to hell in such a way that you actually look forward to the trip. Anonymous

When others walk, run; when others run, walk. Anonymous

True genius sees with the eyes of a child and thinks with the brain of a genie. Puzant Kervork Thomajan

When a true genius appears in this world, you may know him by the sign that the dunces are all in confederacy against him. Jonathan Swift

When I am working on a problem I never think about beauty. I only think about how to solve the problem. But when I have finished, if the solution is not beautiful, I know it is wrong. Buckminster Fuller

ADOPTING A PROBLEM SOLVING ATTITUDE

If you have some problems and obstacles in your life, you're not alone — everyone has them. Much of life's happiness and success depends on being able to prevent these problems, to sidestep them, to minimize them, or to solve them as quickly and effortlessly as possible.

A good starting point is to develop a positive approach to problem-solving, as reflected in some of the following thoughts.

First of all, don't take life so seriously. You're not going to get out of it alive, anyway.

Second, don't take yourself too seriously. Duck the punches if you can; if you can't, roll with them. And, if you can't do that, learn to laugh at yourself.

Third, realize that more than 95% of the things you're worried about and concerned about won't come true anyway. So, relax.

Fourth, understand that life isn't always fair. Sometimes you get the fuzzy end of the lollipop.

Fifth, realize that everybody has problems and obstacles in their life. When it's your turn, don't let it throw you.

Sixth, when you approach those problems, obstacles, and controversies in your life, don't use force, fear, or intimidation as a solution. Oh, you might get your way, but all too often, you'll leave a trail of mistrust, hard feelings, and devastation in your wake. And, using force and intimidation is often a shortsighted approach that will come back to haunt you in the long run.

Instead, solve your problems and eliminate those obstacles through strategies using creativity, tact, and finesse. Not only will you remove those blights from your life with certainty and finality, but, also, you'll be proud of yourself for your ingenuity, and others will marvel at how clever you are.

FINESSIN' EM

There's no precise formula that you can use to solve a problem and reach an expected result. Each situation requires that you craft a unique strategy that is fitting for that problem or obstacle at hand.

Although there is no formula for how to develop finesse, here are some steps and procedures that you can follow to help analyze the problem and develop a creative solution.

1. Gather all of the facts before you attempt to understand the problem or create a solution.

2. Identify what the problem is — what it really is. For instance, if you're short of money, the real problem may be a lack of work effort, a lack of ideas, or poor spending habits.

3. Try to simplify the problem. There may be several fringe issues, but cut to the heart of the matter.

4. Identify the ideal outcome that you would like to see. For example, let's assume you just got fired, and you're mad. What will make you feel better? Severance pay? A good recommendation? Telling the boss off? Getting

even? Decide what you really want before you charge off into action.

5.   Realize there is a solution to your problem or dilemma. It exists. Your job is to find it. The answer may come quickly and easily, or you may need to grind it out over several days or weeks. But it's there.

6.   Use your entire brain in devising a solution. Spend time and effort methodically analyzing the problem and trying to devise a logical solution. As you spend time on the logical (left brain) process, a creative (right brain) answer might come to you in a flash, called the *creative leap*.

   In fact, the more time you spend on the logical process, the more likely you are to devise a creative solution.

   And when trying to devise a creative solution, "sleep on it." That is, as you fall asleep at night, run through your mind everything you know about the problem at hand. All night long, your subconscious mind (the most powerful part of the brain) will mull it over. In the morning, lie still, and think about the problem. Most likely, things will be much clearer, or the entire solution will be there.

7.   There may be more than one viable solution. Consider the ramifications of each before making a decision.

8.   Prepare yourself before putting your plan into action. Rehearse what you're going to say and do. Anticipate all possible outcomes.

9.   Initiate your plan — and, enjoy the results.

The following true stories, scenarios, and essays are examples of how to get what you want through tact, creativity, and finesse. They describe how to get others to stop their bad behavior, how to out-maneuver people in sticky situations, how to handle tricky negotiations and business transactions, how to communicate smoothly and effectively, how to avoid awkward or unpleasant situations, and, if all else fails, how to get even.

When you're faced with life's problems and obstacles, see if you can't come up with a solution similar to some of these. You'll have a lot of fun creating and implementing your plan. And, you'll have a great story that you can tell for the rest of your life.

II.
GETTING THE SCOUNDRELS TO CEASE AND DESIST

Often, your problems or unhappiness are caused by someone other than yourself. It's not fair, but that's the way it is. If you could live your life without dealing with other people, you'd be just fine, but, then, that wouldn't be any fun, either.

So, it looks like we'll be dealing with other people. And, they'll undoubtedly do a few things we won't like. So, we may as well devise some techniques to get the scoundrels to stop what they're doing, so we can have a happier life.

> *When written in Chinese, "crisis" is composed of two characters. One represents danger and the other represents opportunity.* John F. Kennedy

> *Crises bring out the best in the best of us and the worst in the worst of us.* Anonymous

> *No one can make you feel inferior without your consent.* Eleanor Roosevelt.

> *There are two kinds of men who never amount to much: those who cannot do what they are told, and those who can do nothing else.* Cyrus H. Curtis

> *You may be deceived if you trust too much, but you will live in torment if you don't trust enough.* Frank Crane

No one worth possessing can be quite possessed. Sara Teasdale

A man always has two reasons for doing anything — a good reason and the real reason. J.P. Morgan

A reputation once broken may possibly be repaired, but the world will always keep their eyes on the spot where the crack was. Joseph Hall

I discovered I always have choices and sometimes it's only a choice of attitude. Judith M. Knowlton

When your dreams turn to dust, vacuum. Anonymous

Give to a pig when it grunts and a child when it cries, and you will have a fine pig and a bad child. Danish proverb

You may be disappointed if you fail, but you are doomed if you don't try. Beverly Sills

You cannot teach a man anything; you can only help him find it within himself. Galileo

SWEET LIPS

You might call it a fad, or you might call it a fetish. But, most likely, it was simply the "in thing" to do. And, since everybody did it, well, everybody had to do it. And, the harder the authorities tried to stop them, the more they did it, and the harder it was to stop. And the harder it became to stop, the more the authorities knew they had to stop it, just to regain their authority, I suppose.

The problem was, you see, that all the girls at Lincoln High School wore lipstick. And they all applied lipstick about three or four times a day. And they always applied it in the first floor restroom. And, after applying their lipstick, they always blotted it by kissing the mirror. And each tried to outdo the next by making the darkest, roundest, widest, or sexiest kiss. And the custodian, Harriet, had the job of cleaning that restroom every night. And the worst part of the job was cleaning those lipstick kisses off the mirror. And the next night she'd have to do it all over again. Harriet was becoming violently upset over that mirror-kissing fad or fetish or whatever it was, and the more Harriet became upset, the more she demanded the authorities, that being the school administration, do something to stop it. And the more Harriet complained, the harder the administration tried to stop the mirror kissing. The harder they tried to stop it, the worse it got. The worse it got, the madder Harriet got. The madder Harriet got, the more she demanded the administration stop it. The harder the administration tried to stop it, the worse it got. It all just got worse and worse and worse.

Now, the administration really did try to stop the mirror kissing. Even Harriet admitted to that. They posted signs in the restroom and put announcements in the daily bulletin. They asked. They pleaded. They begged. They threatened that anybody caught blotting their lipstick on the mirror would be placed on detention. They sent women teachers into the restroom on sneak attacks to try to catch someone. They threatened to expel anyone caught kissing the mirror. They tried everything, but nothing worked. It just got worse and worse and worse.

And it continued to get worse and worse until one day when Harriet walked into the restroom. The restroom was packed with girls who were talking, laughing, and, of course, applying their lipstick. Now, Harriet had never before encountered the girls face to face, since she always cleaned the restroom at night, after school was out. And, the girls, of course, had never seen Harriet clean the restroom, or the mirror. They simply knew that someone did it, because every morning the restroom was clean, and so was the mirror.

Harriet looked at the lipstick-blotted mirror, shook her head in disgust, and shrugged. She took out her cleaning rag and walked over to a toilet. She dipped the rag in to wet it. Then Harriet walked over to the mirror and began washing off the lipstick kisses. The restroom fell silent. Several girls gasped, and a couple of them gagged.

And, that was the last time that Harriet ever had to wash lipstick kisses off the mirror.

GOOD MORNING, DEA... YIKES!

My friend, Jake, claims this is true. Claims he knows the people involved. Claims it happened about ten years ago.

Ken and Jill had been married for about fifteen years when Jill began to get suspicious. Suspicious that Ken was having an affair. But Jill didn't have any hard evidence, and confronting Ken outright wasn't her style, anyway.

The thing that made Jill particularly suspicious was that after fifteen years at the same job and being home every night, now, all of a sudden, Ken was staying overnight out of town every Wednesday night. The kicker came when Jill found a page from a motel note pad in Ken's pocket — from a motel a scant ten miles from their home.

True to form, the next Wednesday morning, Ken announced that he'd be staying overnight out in the territory.

Just after dark, Jill drove to the motel and carefully checked the parking lot — Ken's car wasn't there. She parked out of sight and waited. At about 11:00 P.M., Ken's car rolled into the parking lot. Ken and a woman got out and entered room 160.

Jill bit her tongue as the lights went out in the motel room — she knew what that meant. She also knew that after having sex, Ken would zonk out and enter a deep sleep resembling a coma. Nothing would wake him.

Jill waited about an hour. Then, she went to the motel office and fabricated a story, although it was mostly true. Her husband was asleep in room 160, and she was locked out, she explained. She needed a key to the room. The desk clerk was happy to oblige.

Jill unlocked the door and eased it open. True to form, in his haste, Ken had failed to lock the security chain.

Jill turned on the bathroom light, which provided enough illumination for her to scan the room. Sure enough, there was Ken zonked out with his floozy lying asleep on the other side of the bed.

Jill quietly tiptoed to the bed and awoke Ken's mistress. "I'm his wife," Jill said firmly. "Take your things, and get the hell out of here."

The mistress was only too happy to comply.

After the mistress left, Jill quietly undressed and slipped into bed beside Ken.

In the morning, Ken awoke, rolled over, and —Yikes!

Jill watched through the slits in her eyes as Ken shot straight up, thumped the side of his head with his hand and shook the cobwebs out of his head. His mouth dropped open, and his eyes darted around the room in panic.

Jill opened her eyes, smiled, and simply said, "Good morning, dear," and rolled over.

Ken didn't ask for an explanation, and Jill didn't offer any. And, neither of them has ever mentioned the incident since.

That was the last time, however, that business kept Ken out of town overnight. Seems staying overnight out in the territory was a nightmare.

HE DIED AND WENT TO WHERE?

I like hanging out with musicians. Also writers and artists. They don't work for a living, they create. And, they're lively, upbeat, colorful, exciting and, perhaps, slightly crazy.

One of my favorite musical friends is a guy named Benny. He's quite a trumpet player — and piano player and saxophone player and trombone player and drummer, and so on. Benny played with a lot of big bands in his day, but when you ask him what his favorite type of music is, he says, "I like all types of music." Besides being a good musician, he's a good diplomat.

Back some years ago, when he was a little younger and still single, Benny traveled the country playing one-nighters. As Benny describes it, there wasn't much to do with your time on the road but to play music, travel, and drink, play music, travel, and drink.

When a group of musicians spend over 300 days a year traveling together on the road, they become pretty close, like a family. They watch out for one another and help each other out, but their methods aren't always orthodox.

Benny tells that on one particularly long and grueling road trip he started to overemphasize the drink part a little heavily. In fact, he would drink when they played music, drink when they traveled, and really guzzle them when the band got down to official serious drinking.

Benny would drink himself into oblivion every night. His buddies in the band would carry him to his hotel room, flop him onto his bed, and he'd sleep there with his clothes on. Benny would awake about noon, jump-start his heart with a couple of bloody Marys and be off on another day of drink, play music, drink, travel, drink, and drink.

Even though most of the guys in the band were more than social drinkers, themselves, and had little room to point fingers, they became concerned about Benny's over-imbibing. For one thing, trumpet players who could also play piano, saxophone, trombone and drums and who were willing to travel were hard to come by. For another thing, Benny was their friend, and he was wasting himself.

Taking Benny aside and talking to him about easing off on the booze wouldn't work, they figured, and it would be out of character for a bunch of roving musicians, anyway. But they had another idea.

Benny was lying on his bed one day, still sleeping, probably about noon. He dreamt that he was hearing singing. It was the

most vivid and real dream he'd ever had. The music seemed to sur-
round and engulf him. It was beautiful. They were singing "Nearer
My God To Thee." Apparently he was dreaming about attending a
funeral.

The singing continued, and slowly it dawned on Benny that it
was real; this was no dream.

He opened his eyelids a slit. Through bleary eyes he could see
all of the members of the band standing around him in a circle.
They were dressed in suits and holding flowers. Their somber
faces continued to sing the beautiful strains of "Nearer My God
To Thee" over and over. Benny slowly felt down with his hand; he
was lying on something soft, made of velvet. He moved his foot a
little to the side, and it pressed against a wall of some sort. He
moved his other foot — another wall. He slowly stretched out his
elbows on both sides of his body, and they, too, pressed against a
wall.

The thought had already crept into his mind, but he refused
to accept it. But now he must. He was in a casket. He was dead.
He was observing his own funeral. He had, no doubt, died from
drinking.

Benny was in the process of telling himself how stupid he had
been to drink so much and vowed, if he had to do it over again,
how he'd limit himself to one or two drinks a day, when the whole
band threw their flowers on top of him.

It so startled Benny that he sat straight up and jumped right
out of the casket, much to the delight of the band members who
were now rolling on the floor in laughter.

Well, that was many years ago, and Benny is still alive. So is his
liver. He made good on his vow, too, pretty good, and became a
moderate drinker and stayed that way.

Like I said, I like musicians and writers and artists. They're
lively, upbeat, colorful, exciting and perhaps, slightly crazy. And,
they are creative.

SPLITTING TENS

The game of blackjack, also called "21," goes like this: The dealer deals two cards to each player and to themself. The players get to see both of their own cards. Only one of the dealer's cards, called the "up card," is visible for all to see; the other card is dealt face down.

The object of the game is for the player to get a higher score than the dealer without "breaking" by going over 21. The player can draw as many additional cards, dealt by the dealer, as they want in their attempt to beat the dealer.

After each player has played their hand by "standing" or "hitting," the dealer turns the hidden card over. If the dealer has 17-21, they must stand. If they have 16 or less, they must hit, and they must continue to hit until they get a total of 17-21 or they break by going over 21.

The player decides to "stand" on their first two cards or to "hit" based upon their point total and the dealer's "up card." In general, if the player has a total of 17-21 on their first two cards, they stand regardless of what the dealer's up card is. If the player has a total of 16 or less, they might stand or hit, depending upon the dealer's up card.

A technique that makes blackjack particularly exciting and potentially profitable is the player's ability to split a matching pair of cards dealt to them, thus making two new hands. For instance, if the player's first two cards are a pair of 8s and the dealer's up card is a 6, the player might split the 8s, making two new hands. In turn, the player would hit each new hand until they eventually stand or break.

There are various strategies for when you should and should not split pairs, based upon what cards are in the pair and, again, what the dealer's up card is.

As you may recall from your math or science classes, an *axiom* is a rule that is *always* true. And, when it comes to splitting pairs, there is one axiom — *Never, ever, never split a pair of 10s or face cards* (which also count ten each). The reasoning is, you have twenty, which is about as good a hand as you can get. If you split this good hand, chances are you'll create two lousy hands and lose them both.

Still, the most violated principle of playing blackjack is splitting pairs of 10s or face cards. And, when someone does it, most of the other players at the table give the splitter a dirty look or shake their heads or just plain get up and leave. Nobody cares whether the splitter wins or loses, of course. What ticks off the other players is that by splitting the pair when they shouldn't have, they draw extra cards they shouldn't have and foul up the rotation of the cards — and (maybe) everybody else's hand. So, if you play blackjack, remember the axiom — Never, ever, never split a pair of 10s or face cards.

End of the blackjack lesson — now for the story.

I was sitting at a blackjack table in Las Vegas with five other players when a guy split a pair of 10s against the dealer's up card, which was an 8. A couple of players shook their heads in disgust, one mumbled something under his breath about being an idiot, and another got up and stomped away from the table.

But, an attractive lady in her mid thirties handled it a little differently. She turned her head and looked that splitter squarely in the eye and said with a touch of sarcasm in her voice, "If you had a twenty-inch dick, would you cut that in half, too?"

Well, the guy almost croaked — but, he never split another pair of 10s while he was at the table, and I'll bet he never does again!

RING, RING

Laura had lived in her home for many years and had the same telephone number for all that time.

A developer built a brand new motel-convention center-banquet facility and selected a phone number that was just one digit different from Laura's.

Immediately after the motel opened, Laura started getting a flood of phone calls intended for the motel. They came in the early morning, they came late at night, and they came all day long in-between. At first it was a little amusing. Then it became irritating. Then it got so bothersome that it entirely disrupted Laura's life.

Laura contacted the motel, explained the problem, and asked them to change their phone number. They refused; saying it would be too costly, since they'd also have to reprint their letterheads and invoices. She called them again and again, but the motel management had no empathy for her situation. The best solution they could offer was that Laura should change *her* phone number.

Laura, having become a little stubborn by this time, refused. After all, she had the phone number first.

The misdialed phone calls, Laura's exasperation, and the motel management's disinterest continued. Finally, one day, Laura had had enough.

The phone rang and Laura answered.

"Is this the Anchor Inn?" the voice asked.

"Yes, it is," Laura answered, "How may I help you?"

"Do you have four rooms available for Friday and Saturday night, October 21 and 22?"

"Yes, we do." Laura replied, and went ahead and booked the four rooms.

Over the course of the next several weeks, Laura continued to book rooms — and wedding receptions, and banquets, and more rooms. She booked a couple of dozen Christmas parties and a half dozen New Year's eve parties. She booked a couple of sweet-sixteen parties and two huge conventions. She booked and booked.

Towards the end of October, the impact started to hit the motel. By Thanksgiving, the impact had hit it like a sledgehammer. By mid December, the motel changed its phone number. By mid January, the motel was in such chaos and was under the crush of so many lawsuits that it was forced to close.

And now Laura has what she always wanted — just a little peace and quiet, free from that doggone ringing noise all the time.

GUESS WHO

Here's an idea that's dirty, low-down, tricky, sneaky, and under-handed. You'll just love it.

It didn't start out that way, though, for Larissa. Her motives were genuine and honest; her intentions, pure.

You see, Larissa read this article in a magazine about how to put some romance and spark back into your marriage. It was just what Larissa needed, since lately her husband, Terry, had been so busy at work that he didn't have the time or the strength to pay much attention to her.

The article said you've got to be creative. Do something unex-pected. Break the mold. Color outside of the lines. Be daring. Be creative. Do something tantalizing. Be the instigator.

Larissa thought about all that for awhile and, finally, came up with a plan. She went to the card shop and carefully selected just the perfect card. Then, she went home and cut words and names out of the daily newspaper which, together, spelled her husband's name and work address. She meticulously glued them on the envelope and had to admit that it probably looked exactly the way a ransom note would look. It was bound to get his attention. It would pique his interest. It would be the one letter in his stack that he would just have to open.

Then, Larissa cut more words out of the newspaper to spell out the message that she wanted on the card. She glued the mes-sage in place and sat back and admired her work. It was perfect. If that message, "From Your Secret Admirer," didn't propel him straight home from work, nothing would.

Larissa mailed the card to her husband at his office on Wednesday afternoon, and the postal clerk assured her that it would reach its destination the next day.

Now, for the second part of the plan to rekindle the romance. On Thursday evening, Larissa cooked Terry's favorite meal and dressed in a casual but, nevertheless, sexy outfit. The article had said not to overdo it and not to be too obvious, or the man might feel he's being manipulated or simply being "used" as a sex object. (Hey, don't blame me, I'm just repeating what it said.)

Larissa checked the clock — 5:30. Terry should be home any minute. She checked it again, 6:00 — he should be there soon. She checked again, 6:30 — something must have held him up at work. Finally at about 6:45, he pulled into the driveway.

Larissa gathered herself and thought back to what that maga-zine article had said — if you're making secret plans that you haven't told your husband about, don't be upset if he doesn't follow your time schedule. Good advice, Larissa decided as she prepared to put the rest of the plan into action. She was especially eager to see what Terry's reaction was to the "Secret Admirer" card she'd sent him.

Terry entered the house like usual, kissed Larissa on the cheek like usual, apologized for being tied up at work like usual, asked what was for dinner like usual, and settled into his recliner to read the paper like usual. He didn't even notice her sexy outfit — maybe she had understated it a little too much.

During dinner, Larissa asked Terry if anything important had happened at work today and he replied, "Nothing special."

Damn that postal clerk, her card never arrived today. Or, maybe it was the company mailroom that was to blame. Well, whoever was to blame had just ruined her romantic evening. Somehow the magazine article hadn't mentioned what to do if the plan unraveled.

So, as usual, Larissa washed dishes while Terry fell asleep in front of the TV. Some romantic evening.

The following evening, Terry again came home from work late. Larissa was eager to see what he thought of her "Secret Admirer" card. Surely, it would have been delivered by now. Terry never brought it up.

Finally, when dinner was about half over, Larissa asked, "Did you happen to get a special card in the mail at work?"

Terry blurted out without thinking, "That was from *you*?"

"Who did you think it was from?" Larissa asked.

Terry stammered and stuttered, trying to create some plausible explanation, but it was obvious that he was grasping at straws and failing miserably.

The thought had never entered Larissa's mind before, but it did now.

"Are you having an affair?" she asked.

Terry looked straight at her, and she could see the blood drain from his face as tears began to well up in his eyes.

The magazine article sure as hell didn't say anything about this happening.

Well, that was a couple of years ago, and, as it turned out, it was the bitter medicine that it took to get both Larissa and Terry to face their problems and to work together to solve them. Today, they're a happy, attentive, loving couple, and Larissa no longer needs to resort to "Secret Admirer" cards to catch Terry's attention. And, she no longer reads magazine articles about how to put romance and life back into your marriage.

So, there you have it. A surefire way to put a little spark into your romance — or to find out if your lover has some action going on the side. But, before you go ahead and send your lover a "Secret Admirer" card, be sure that you want to know the answer.

SPRINGING THE TRAP DOOR

Miss Holmquist was strict. You were expected to attend her English classes at Riverside College. You see, she had this crazy idea that students who attended classes regularly learned more and earned higher grades than those whose attendance was sporadic.

She accepted no lame stories about cars that wouldn't start, flat tires, alarm clocks that didn't go off, or friends who forgot to pick you up. Excuses — she'd heard them all, from the student who claimed to have buried four grandmothers in a single semester to the student who swore that he'd been abducted by aliens.

Yeah, she'd seen it all until, that is, Jerome Adams signed up for her class. Jerome's specialty was telephone excuses. One call, for example, came from a man who identified himself as Jerome's father, who said he was calling from his home in Milwaukee. He asked that Jerome be excused from missing classes the previous week since he had called Jerome home to help bail flood water out of the basement — in the winter. It was amazing, Miss Holmquist thought, how youthful Jerome's father sounded.

Then, there was the phone call from Jerome's mother — a squeaky sounding woman whose voice would occasionally slip in a baritone note now and then. She asked that Jerome be excused from classes for the next two weeks, because she was about to fall down and break a leg and would need his help to get around.

And, there was that call from the sheriff describing how Jerome was involved in dangerous undercover work that had him stressed out. The sheriff said that all of his teachers should appreciate Jerome's risking his life for society and that they should give him high grades, especially in English.

Jerome's crowning touch, though, was triggered by the Hepatitis A scare that was going around campus. You see, three students at one of the local high schools had contracted Hepatitis A, and, although there were no reported cases at the college, officials were fearful that it might hit campus. Therefore, to head it off, the college informed students of the potential health problem and posted signs all over the restrooms saying to make sure to wash hands with soap and hot water to reduce the risk of contacting or spreading Hepatitis A.

That Hepatitis A scare was all Jerome needed to set his plan into motion.

The phone rang at the college office — it was the health officer from the medical clinic. Jerome Adams had come down with

Hepatitis A — please excuse him from all classes for last week and next week, the speaker said. Just for good measure, the health officer also called Miss Holmquist and left her a special message saying how terribly sick Jerome really was and how she should have sympathy and understanding.

About a week and a half later, Jerome finally showed up, and Miss Holmquist called him to the front of the room. She stayed back several feet from Jerome and talked in a hushed voice. Nevertheless, the rest of the students could still overhear her.

She was so sorry that Jerome had come down with Hepatitis A, Miss Holmquist explained sympathetically, and she hoped that he would fully recover soon. Jerome wallowed in the sympathy.

Then Miss Holmquist asked Jerome if he knew that Hepatitis A was highly contagious. Yes, he did. Then she asked if he knew that he could spread the germs for up to three weeks after he felt he was cured of the disease. No, Jerome admitted, he didn't know that.

Miss Holmquist calmly reached into a desk drawer and pulled out a pair of rubber gloves and asked Jerome to put them on. He did. Then she directed all of the students to move to one side of the classroom and moved a lone chair to the far side of the room for Jerome, where she had him sit all by himself.

Jerome had unwittingly positioned himself squarely in the center of a trap door, so to speak, and Miss Holmquist pulled the lever. Boom, he dropped like a sack of potatoes.

I'd like to tell you that this little incident straightened Jerome out and that he eventually became the president of General Motors. It didn't, and he didn't. But, it was the last time that Jerome, or any of his relatives, the sheriff, the health officer, or anyone else ever called Miss Holmquist to tell her to excuse Jerome Adams from class.

You see, Miss Holmquist had this crazy idea that students who attended classes regularly learned more and earned higher grades than those who attended sporadically.

TIMBER!

Jim and Judy are fortunate enough to own two homes. "Home home" is the permanent place where they've got all of their stuff. Their "second home" is a condo at the lake.

If you've ever lived in a condo, you're chuckling already. If you haven't lived in one, you've missed one of life's rare experiences. Not necessarily a good experience or a bad experience — just a rare one.

You see, if you live in a condo, you can't do anything unless everybody votes on it first. But the vote doesn't come until after the arguing, name-calling, and swearing. You don't paint the exterior, plant trees, build a fence, hire a guy to mow the lawn, fix the leaking roof, or boycott the neighborhood tavern until everybody has had their say.

Jim and Judy's condo building is a small one — just sixteen units. But, with a husband and wife per unit, that's thirty-two different opinions at a minimum, and often more. Jim recalls one issue on which there were at least fifty different opinions — from thirty-two people.

If you've lived in a condo, you already know all this. If you haven't, please trust me and accept it as fact.

After many debates, it was decided to enlarge the cement patios on the lakeside of Jim and Judy's building. In order to do so, the four large, evergreen trees along the front of the building would have to be removed. Since they had gotten out of hand and looked like hell, anyway, that created no controversy.

The trees were removed and the concrete patio was poured. The patio looked very nice, everybody agreed — honest.

The condo association has about ten committees to work on various projects, one of which is the Building and Grounds Committee. This committee can spend up to $500 on needed improvements without an official vote of the group. It's usually wise to bring it up for a vote first, anyway, or they'll surely catch hell later, even if they are technically within the rules.

So, after the cement patios were poured, the Building and Grounds Committee purchased and planted four new evergreens to replace the four that had been removed to make room for the new patios. The trees cost $50 each — a total of $200. Well within their budget. And, one would probably assume, the old trees would be replaced with new ones after the new patios were built, anyway. So, no problem with planting four new trees. Right?

Wrong. When one of the owners showed up for a leisurely weekend at the lake and saw the new trees, he went berserk. He ranted that someone might hide behind one of the trees at night and jump out and attack his wife. That had never been raised as a problem before when they had the old evergreens that stood ten feet high and were four feet wide, but the new trees standing three feet high and one foot wide seemed to pose this problem. He also thought that the trees cost too much, that they would steal moisture from the lawn, and that they weren't color coordinated well enough with the blue exterior of the building. Likewise, he was upset that he didn't get to vote on whether or not the new trees should be planted, which was probably the main problem — he wanted to vote. Most likely, had there been a vote, he would have voted for planting the trees — after the arguing and swearing was all over. Such is life in a condo.

When they awoke on Saturday morning, Jim and Judy learned there had been a murder. The two evergreens from the end of the building where Berserk Guy lived had been sawed off and were lying on a picnic table. Now, no one says Berserk Guy, did it, but you be the judge.

In true condo fashion, somebody had called the cops, who were conducting an investigation. Berserk Guy was fingered as a likely suspect, but he denied it. He was not given a lie detector test. The crime remains unsolved to this day.

The next week, the Building and Grounds Committee purchased two more evergreens for $50 each and planted them where the two murdered trees had been.

The next weekend, Berserk Guy showed up again and rumor had it that he had commented to a bartender at the neighborhood tavern that he would cut down the new trees and that he would keep cutting down the new trees as long as there were new trees. He and his companion, Mr. Budweiser, would do this.

This tree business was starting to get expensive, at $50 a crack, and it looked like they might go through a whole forest before Berserk Guy quit or the Buildings and Grounds Committee gave in. There was no reasoning with Berserk Guy and you couldn't guard the trees twenty-four hours a day.

Jim decided to try a different approach. He typed a short note on a 3 by 5 card and encased it in plastic. At about 2:00 A.M., Jim snuck down and tied the note to the tree outside Berserk Guy's patio using fishing line.

When Jim arose in the morning, the tree was still there, and so was the note, flapping gently in the wind.

That was more than three years ago and the trees are still there and doing nicely. Jim retrieved the note one early morning, and it's in his scrapbook.

Oh, the note. It said, "This tree has been chemically treated. If you cut it down, your penis will fall off."

Gone Fishin'

Mike always looked forward to his annual fishing trip with gusto. So much so, in fact, that his wife, Sandy, became a little suspicious. The fact that Mike never brought any fish home was just one of the things that didn't seem to add up.

As usual, Mike and his buddies took off for their annual fishing trip the first week in June.

When Mike returned home, he described to Sandy the great time they'd had fishing, fishing, fishing. From sunup to sundown, fishing, fishing, fishing.

Then Mike asked how come Sandy hadn't packed any underwear for his weeklong trip. To which Sandy walked over to Mike's tackle box and opened it up to reveal several pair of underwear stacked neatly on top of his fishing gear.

It seems after that particular fishing trip Mike kind of lost interest in fishing, and Sandy's happy to have a handyman around to help with the yard work that first week in June.

ONE MAN'S JUNK IS ANOTHER MAN'S TREASURE

Ken Evans owns and operates a restaurant. The front of the restaurant faces a busy street. The street behind the restaurant is residential, lined with older, two-story houses.

Ken generally takes the garbage out to the dumpster behind his building at about 11:00 P.M. each night. He began to notice that on Thursday nights there were extra bags of garbage in his dumpster. He sifted through one of the bags and identified it as normal household trash. Apparently, one of the neighbors from the houses behind his building was using his dumpster to dispose of their household garbage. Ken was curious.

The next Thursday night, Ken watched his dumpster from a darkened back room of the restaurant. At precisely 9:30, a woman emerged from the row of houses with two huge plastic bags of garbage. She snuck up to the dumpster, looked around for witnesses, and threw the bags in.

Ken watched his dumpster the next Thursday night and the next and the next. On eight consecutive Thursdays, at precisely 9:30 P.M., the same woman deposited two huge bags of garbage in his dumpster.

This had been going on for nearly three months, now, and Ken estimated she had deposited enough garbage to fill two dumpsters. And Ken was paying to have it hauled away.

Although Ken actually enjoyed the game — watching the woman sneak up to his dumpster, throw the garbage in, and hustle back to her house — he decided to end it.

At 9:25 the next Thursday night, Ken took his place.

Sure enough, at precisely 9:30, the woman approached the dumpster with her two bags of garbage. She looked around, saw no witnesses, and made her deposit.

Ken stepped from the shadows about six feet from the woman. He held out his opened billfold and said calmly, "How much do I owe you for that?"

Ken's Thursday nights aren't nearly as much fun as they used to be.

SLEEP TIGHT

There were eight of them going on the overnight business trip — seven old salts and the new guy, Charlie.

Since the company was, shall we say, conservative, four rooms with two beds each were booked. Two men would share a room.

Sharing rooms really wasn't a problem, except for one thing. One of the guys, George, was known as a world-class snorer. Those who had shared a room with George in the past claimed that he sounds like a cross between a locomotive and a jet engine. And no one who ever shared a room with George ever got a moment's sleep. But that really wasn't a problem, either. The old salts simply decided to stick the new guy, Charlie, with George.

The old salts had a lot of fun ribbing Charlie about how he'd never sleep a wink and about how he'd need to prop his eyes open with toothpicks at the next day's meeting.

The plan was to meet for breakfast in the hotel coffee shop at 7:00 A.M. They were all there except for George and Charlie. Momentarily, Charlie arrived without George.

The others were eager to hear Charlie's version of what it was like to spend a night listening to George's snoring.

Surprisingly, Charlie looked well rested and sharp — unlike the way any of them had felt the morning after spending a sleepless night as George's roommate.

Yes, he had slept well, Charlie said.

No, George didn't snore at all.

No, Charlie hadn't worn earplugs.

No, Charlie hadn't covered his head with a pillow.

Yes, Charlie had a secret of how he did it.

When they had gone to bed the night before, Charlie had turned off the light and walked over to the bed where George lie. He bent down, kissed George on the forehead, and crawled into his own bed. He never heard a peep from George all night.

III.
IF YOU CAN'T BEDAZZLE 'EM WITH BRILLIANCE, BAFFLE 'EM WITH BULLSHIT

There are times when we won't be able to outrun them and we won't be able to hide. So, we'll have to outmaneuver them with some fancy footwork.

Lots of folks confuse bad management with destiny. Kim Hubbard

Vision without action is a daydream. Action without vision is a nightmare. Japanese proverb

There are two ways of meeting difficulties. You alter the difficulties or you alter yourself to meet them. Phyllis Botteme

What men prize most is privilege, even if it be that of chief mourner at a funeral. James Russell Lowell

The weak can never forgive. Forgiveness is the attribute of the strong. Mahatma Gandi

If I had eight hours to chop down a tree, I'd spend six hours sharpening my ax. Abraham Lincoln

It's not whether you really cry. It's whether the audience thinks you're crying. Ingrid Bergman

If you see a tennis player who looks as if he is working hard, then that means he isn't very good. Helen Willis Moody

> *The best way to convince a fool that he is wrong is to let him have his own way.* Josh Billings

> *If you want to fool the world, tell the truth.* Otto von Bismarck

BUDDY, CAN YOU SPARE ME A DIME?

Johnny Jenkins was a ne'er-do-well. Some people called him a bum. But Johnny liked to make people believe that he had money. Sometimes he even *did* have money. He was a panhandler.

One day, Johnny had $200 in his pocket. He was walking down a bad street in Chicago and noticed a gang of young hoodlums shuffling towards him on the other side of the street. Johnny was street-wise enough to know what was going to happen. In a moment, the young thugs would cross the street, mug him, and take his money. If he turned and ran, they'd give chase, catch him, and probably beat him worse for his trouble.

Johnny had an idea. He boldly crossed the street and approached the gang of youths. He held a shaking hand out to them, palm up.

"Can you spare me a quarter, please," Johnny begged.

Surprisingly, one of the youths gave him a quarter.

"Now get the hell out of here, you bum," the young thug ordered.

Johnny obeyed, hustling down the street. He had avoided his beating — and he still had his $200 in his pocket, and twenty-five cents.

MILITARY STRATEGIES

My friend, Sam, claims that this happened to him and his pal, Ed, when they were in college.

It was their senior year, and they were registering for their final semester. They signed up for the remaining courses to complete their majors, and they each needed one elective course to round out their schedules and to earn enough credits to graduate.

Sam and Ed had questioned dozens of acquaintances, seeking the easiest course on campus for that elective they had to take. One course was recommended time and again, "Take American History from Professor Peterson." "Take American History from Professor Peterson." "Take American History from Professor Peterson ...."

It wasn't that American History was such an easy topic that earned the course the reputation as the easiest course on campus. Nor was it that Professor Peterson indiscriminately gave everyone who signed up for the course an A. The thing that earned the course its reputation was that Professor Peterson asked only one essay question on the final exam. And Professor Peterson, who was a real military buff, always asked the same essay question on the final exam. For years and years and years, the same question: "Discuss the military strategies of General Douglas MacArthur."

A student's final grade was based on that one essay question and nothing more. And Professor Peterson always gave great lectures and great handouts on the military strategies of General Douglas MacArthur. So, it was pretty easy to do a good job on the test with a minimal amount of study effort.

Sam and Ed had a great time that semester. They attended Professor Peterson's American History class only a few times, but had secured the lecture notes and handouts on the military strategies of General Douglas MacArthur.

The night before the American History course final exam, Sam and Ed barricaded themselves in their room to study the military strategies of General Douglas MacArthur. They studied and quizzed each other and studied some more until they could discuss the strategies forwards and backwards.

Sam and Ed entered the classroom for the American History final exam with an abundance of confidence. They had an A in the bag.

Professor Peterson handed out the test booklet, which consisted of a title page, a single question on page two and several blank pages for the student answers. He instructed the class to not look at the question on page two until everyone received their test booklets, so everyone could start on the exam at the same time.

"Now turn to page two, read the question carefully, and answer it as completely as you can," instructed Professor Peterson. "You have a two-hour time limit."

All forty students in the class turned to page two at the same time — and then there was a collective gasp.

Sam read the question again and he stared at it in disbelief. "Criticize President Dwight D. Eisenhower's inaugural address."

About two-thirds of the class, including Ed, simply wrote their names on the tests and handed them in blank. The rest gave a half-hearted attempt at creating their own version of the inaugural address and turned in a hope and a prayer that might get them a D if they were lucky.

Fifteen minutes after the exam started; the room was empty except for two people, Professor Peterson and Sam.

Sam wrote on and on feverishly. For a half-hour he wrote, for an hour, for an hour and a half. He asked Professor Peterson for extra paper, and he wrote until just shortly before the two-hour time limit expired.

Professor Peterson posted the final grades the next day. About two-thirds of the class, including Ed, failed. About a third of the class, those who turned in the hope and prayer, got Ds. There was only one A — Sam.

How did Sam miraculously earn his A? Well, with a little ingenuity. Here's the first paragraph from his essay exam.

"Let those who feel they must, go ahead and criticize our distinguished and beloved President. As for me, I prefer to discuss the military strategies of General Douglas MacArthur."

THE DEMONSTRATION

It was the tenth time in the past two weeks that the vacuum cleaner salesman had called asking to — begging to — come over to John and Lynn's house to demonstrate his vacuum cleaner. Not only to demonstrate it, but also to demonstrate how it could pick up a steel ball. In fact, he seemed obsessed with wanting to suck up that steel ball.

Finally, John and Lynn caved in and agreed to the demonstration and sales presentation. But they were dreading it. They knew that this pushy, shovey, overbearing salesman wouldn't take no for an answer. And, if they didn't buy this time, he'd hound them time and time again until they gave up and bought just to get rid of him.

But, John had a plan.

The vacuum salesman, Leo, showed up five minutes early for his 7:00 P.M. appointment — talk about eager. He was full of enthusiasm and fire and was bragging, again, about how they'd be amazed at how his vacuum cleaner could pick up a steel ball.

With great fanfare, Leo unpacked his demonstration unit and asked John to plug it into a wall outlet. Always a good idea to involve the prospect in some little task that they can handle, you know.

John eagerly grabbed the cord and marched over to an outlet at the far side of the room and plugged it in.

With a little smirk on his face and a cocky air, Leo brought out the steel ball and placed it on the floor in front of his vacuum cleaner. He reached down with his foot and flicked on the switch of his cleaner and the cleaner kicked on, making a low, dull roar.

The smirk and cockiness disappeared from Leo's face like someone had hit him in the face with a shovel. He looked at the machine — he looked at the hose — he looked back at the machine. This mighty steel-ball-sucking-machine was supposed to make a sound like a jet engine, and here it sounded like a wounded meat grinder. No power, no high-pitched whir, no guts.

Leo tried everything, but nothing worked — he couldn't even get his vacuum to pick up a few scraps of shredded paper, let alone a steel ball.

Finally, in frustration, Leo gave up. He packed up his prized vacuum cleaner, his steel ball, and his pride and wimped out the door. All without even discovering that John had plugged his vacuum into an outlet with a wall switch. A wall switch with a rheostat (dimmer switch) on it. A rheostat that was turned down to half power.

Maybe a little sneaky — but highly effective. And Leo never did call back.

THE STROLL

Tom and I worked for the same company. His office was just down the hall and around the corner from mine, and wherever I went took me past his door.

If Tom had the door shut and was working, I would pass by without stopping in. If his door was open and he was working, I would pass by and simply say, "Hello, Tom." If his door was open and he, seemingly, wasn't working, I'd often stop in for a little chat — weekend plans, the football team, office gossip, dreams and schemes — anything but anything to do with work. I certainly enjoyed these little dalliances, and I'm sure Tom did, too.

I recall one time I passed Tom's office. The door was open, and he, seemingly, wasn't working. So I stopped in to chitchat. I don't recall what we were talking about — nothing much, I'm sure. What I do recall is this — Tom and I chatting, walking down the hallway.

"How did I get out here?" I asked myself.

A moment ago I was in Tom's office chatting with him, and, now, without my even realizing it had happened, here we were out in the hallway.

When we came to the intersection of another hallway, I continued on the errand that had been temporarily interrupted by the stop at Tom's office, and Tom went the other way.

When I returned about a minute later, Tom was back in his office, door shut, working.

I was a little embarrassed. Apparently, even though Tom seemingly wasn't working when I stopped in, he was. And I had interrupted him, and he had eased me out of his office so smoothly that I didn't even know it had happened. I was intrigued by exactly how he had done that without my knowing it and was determined to find out. It was a good technique.

From time to time, just as before, I continued to stop by Tom's office for a chat, if the door was open and he, seemingly, wasn't working. Most of those times, I'm sure, he actually wasn't working, and he enjoyed the short break as much as I did.

But one day, it finally happened. Tom's door was open, and he, seemingly, wasn't working. So I stopped in. Tom chatted graciously for a couple of minutes, seeming to enjoy it very much. Then, when it was apparently time for me to go, Tom rolled his chair back away from his desk and slowly stood up, talking to me all the while. He continued to talk to me as he nonchalantly picked up his coffee cup and slowly walked around his desk. Soon, he was beside me, and we were talking. Then we were both walking — through his office door and out into the hallway. And we continued to walk and talk until we came to the intersection of the other hallway and parted ways. Smooth. Tom was smooth.

I hurried down the hallway to complete my errand. I checked my watch as I approached Tom's office on my return trip — a little over a minute. Sure enough, Tom's door was closed, and he was in there, working.

I admired Tom's technique. Instead of flat-out telling me that he was too busy to chat or letting me hang around as long as I might, he simply eased me out of his office. And then he went back to work. He didn't throw cold water on our interesting chats or on our friendship, and he didn't let me ruin his workday, either.

After that, I became more considerate of Tom's time and, I guess, of everyone else's time, too. Oh, I still stopped in to see Tom just like always, but I paid more attention to reading the signs that told me if he was in a chatting mood or not. And, he never had to ease me out of his office again.

I would chuckle, though, every time I'd see Tom walk out of his office with someone, coffee cup in hand, and watch them stroll down the hallway. I knew exactly what Tom was doing. I wonder if anyone else ever figured it out.

P-A-T-I-E-N-C-E

My uncle, Fred, is a world traveler who makes at least one foreign excursion per year and has done so for over fifty years. One of his favorite destinations is Germany, since he is of German ancestry. He speaks German like a native and knows a great deal about German heritage and customs.

One Christmas Eve about four years ago, there was a knock on the front door of Fred's house. He opened the door and was greeted by a German-speaking Santa Claus. They conversed in German for a few moments, and Santa gave Fred a present — a bottle of his favorite bourbon. Santa bid him *gut nacht* and left — without revealing who he was or who sent him.

About three years later at a family gathering, my cousin, Charles, asked Fred if he ever found out who sent that German-speaking Santa Claus.

"Not until right now," Uncle Fred said with a wry smile on his face.

You see, Fred never told anyone about the incident, knowing that some day the perpetrator would just have to bring it up — and reveal themselves in the process. It took three years, but Uncle Fred's patience was rewarded.

Similar occurrences happen to each of us throughout life. The normal tendency is to try to figure out who did it or to accuse enough people until someone finally takes the credit — or the blame.

Next time somebody pulls an anonymous prank on you, keep your mouth shut — forever, if necessary. Undoubtedly, the prankster will be so curious that they'll just have to ask you about it or will have to comment on it — a confession as certain and solid as one signed, sealed and delivered.

MAKE YOURSELF AT HOME

A woman in her eighties who lived alone was awakened early one morning by a sound in her living room. She said a quick prayer, got dressed, and went to investigate.

Sure enough, a stranger was rummaging through her desk, looking for valuables. Thinking quickly, she greeted the man as though she had mistaken him for a close friend of her son. She even told him to make himself at home while she made him some coffee and breakfast. After all, she explained, her son wouldn't arrive for at least another two hours.

The burglar bought the story hook, line, and sinker, believing, no doubt, that she was not only old, but that she also had bad vision and was senile to boot.

Thus, he allowed her to ramble around the house at will and didn't object when she said she had to go to her bedroom to take her medicine. When out of his sight, she turned on the television set and calmly telephoned police.

She then returned to the kitchen and poured the burglar a cup of coffee and dished up his breakfast. She told him she was going to have her morning coffee on the front porch, that he should make himself at home and to call her if he needed anything.

When the police arrived, the burglar was just finishing breakfast, and the woman was cooly and calmly enjoying her cup of coffee on the front porch as she did every morning.

This is a true story, by the way, and it proves that tact and creativity know no bounds because of age, physical health, or other limitations that a person might have.

The Gentleman

You already know the background for this story, since it was one of the most highly publicized stories in the history of the world. Let me summarize the important elements, anyway, just to get the chronology straight, since that is very important for the observation we're about to make.

President Bill Clinton was accused of sexual harassment by Paula Jones for alleged rude, crude, and lewd comments and actions he made toward her while he was governor of Arkansas.

Eventually, the lawsuit headed toward a trial, and President Clinton was subpoenaed to testify. By this time, rumors of some type of a sexual relationship between President Clinton and a White House intern, Monica Lewinsky, had surfaced.

If the rumors were true, this would place the President in a very precarious situation. If he admitted to it during his Paula Jones testimony, it would almost certainly cement Jones's case against him. On the other hand, if he, in fact, did have an affair with Ms. Lewinsky and denied it in his testimony, he ran the risk of the truth coming out later and of his being found guilty of perjury.

Now, admitting to an affair or being found guilty of sexual harassment would be embarrassing, but it probably wouldn't result in his being impeached. Lying under oath about an affair with Ms. Lewinsky, however, would be perjury, and that's an impeachable offense.

As you will recall, in his testimony in the Paula Jones case and in statements he made publicly, President Clinton vehemently denied any improper relationship with Ms. Lewinsky. Of course, at the time of these statements, none of us, including the President, knew what revelations about the matter might be later made public by Ms. Lewinsky or by others.

Some time after President Clinton's testimony, Ms. Lewinsky worked out a deal with prosecutors that she would tell the whole truth about her relationship with President Clinton in return for their agreement not to prosecute her. And, as we all know, she admitted to having an ongoing affair with the President that included numerous encounters.

President Clinton was, again, in a very precarious position. He could now admit to the affair and admit he lied under oath and basically indict himself for perjury, or he could continue to deny the affair and call Ms. Lewinsky a liar. As we can see, his position wasn't only precarious, he was trapped.

As you'll recall, he continued to deny the affair. Subsequently, Linda Tripp's tapes of secretly recorded conversations with Ms. Lewinsky, where she repeatedly discussed her affair with the President, were made public. These tapes served to collaborate Ms. Lewinsky's testimony and to contradict the President's version.

As you know, President Clinton's alleged lying under oath and the subsequent chain of events were primary reasons why the House of Representatives impeached him.

All of this may have been avoidable, however. It appears that President Clinton had one golden opportunity to change his version of the story after Ms. Lewinsky testified that she and the President had had an affair, in direct contradiction to his previous testimony. And, it appears that he may have been able to do it in such a manner that the public might not only have forgiven him, but actually admired him. And, it may have so disarmed the House of Representatives that they may have refused to impeach him, because they understood the reason for his false testimony and forgave him for it.

So here's what he could have done. Let's start with a quick review of the chain of events:

1. President Clinton testifies in the Paula Jones suit and denies having an affair with Ms. Lewinsky.

2. Ms. Lewinsky testifies and says that she did have an affair with the President.

3. Now it's President Clinton's turn to testify, again, and to address the American public.

At this point President Clinton should have realized that the cat was out of the bag and, no matter how strongly he might deny the affair, various forms of proof (like gifts and witnesses) did exist that could easily contradict it. Thus, continuing to deny the affair would only get him in deeper. But suddenly changing his story and admitting the affair would still leave him open to the charge of perjury.

Such a dilemma. What to do? Well, here's an idea that had a good chance of working. After Ms. Lewinsky admitted to the affair, President Clinton could have boldly made a public statement similar to this:

"My fellow Americans. I was raised in the south to be a Southern Gentleman. A Southern Gentleman never talks about a relationship with a woman until the woman talks about the relationship first. That's the code of a Southern Gentleman. That is why, when I testified in the Paula Jones case, I was honor-bound to deny a relationship with Ms. Lewinsky. Since that time, however, she had chosen to publicly admit to the relationship. Therefore, I am now free to admit to it as well. I hope you do not blame me for trying to follow the code of being a Southern Gentleman. Good night, and God bless."

Well, it was worth a try. And you've got to admit it's a whole lot more ingenious (or, at least, no less ridiculous) than the various approaches concocted by that battery of White House lawyers.

STRAIGHT OUT OF THE MOVIES

True story. A woman called the police. She explained that she and some friends had been having a party. Along about midnight, one of the partygoers, her brother-in-law, had turned into a werewolf. Really, an honest-to-goodness werewolf.

He began growling and howling and jumping from one piece of furniture to another. Then he began drooling, and then he attacked and bit two of the other partygoers. They had tried to overpower him, but he had developed superhuman strength and could not be subdued. He had escaped from the house and was on the loose outdoors.

When the police arrived, the partygoer-turned-werewolf was sitting on the top of a car baying at the moon. Instead of shooting the werewolf, as the plot of a good Grade B movie might require, the police cowed him into submission by barking at him. Now, that's finesse!

MUSIC TO MY EARS

My friend, Harry, operates a nightclub where he occasionally hires live bands to perform. Through the years, Harry has experimented with a wide variety of bands, trying to find just the right one that would draw in a crowd. Big crowds, of course, translate into big cover charge income, and, also into big beverage sales.

Now, if it were up to Harry, he'd bring in an opera or a symphony, because that's where his personal music tastes lie. But you'd never even pay the phone bill with a nightclub act like that. Not in the nightclub Harry runs. Not with Harry's clientele.

Finally, after trying all sorts of bands, Harry stumbled onto one that his clientele liked. Hell, they didn't like them, they *loved* them. They went wild over them. Nutso.

But, much to Harry's chagrin, this was a punk-grunge type band that was about as far from Harry's personal musical tastes as you can get. One band member had a mohawk (but it was kind of off center), another had a bowl-type haircut (that really showcased his pink hair), another had body piercing all over his eyebrows, forehead, ears, nose, and tongue (and who knew where else), and the band leader had all this leather and chains and wore high-heeled shoes and had on some type of makeup that looked like pancake mix.

When the band played, they would all of a sudden just crash into each other or jump on top of one another. And when the crowd danced, they'd bang into each other and spit on each other — and everybody loved it. I was there, and it was quite a show. I didn't get in on the dancing, but I did spit back at one guy.

The band quit playing at 1:30 A.M. — in plenty of time to clear the place out before the state's mandatory 2:00 A.M. closing time. But the crowd wouldn't leave, not one of them. They just kept on dancing and crashing into each other and spitting on everyone.

Finally, when it was about ten minutes to 2:00, Harry's huge doorman tried to herd them out the door, but nobody would budge. Next, Harry got on the microphone and pleaded with them — still nobody would go.

At about one minute to 2:00, the crowd was still going strong, and Harry was in jeopardy of losing his license. Then, inspiration hit him. Harry grabbed one of his opera tapes and popped it into the cassette player and turned up the volume. In Harry's own words, "They cleared outta there in about seventeen seconds."

This might be called the "What's good for the goose is good for the gander" strategy or "The hair of the dog that bit you" strategy or the "Harry, you can take your earplugs out now" technique.

But whatever you call it, it proves, once again, that one man's dessert is another man's poison, and vice versa.

Perceptions

It was a hot grounder hit to the shortstop's right. He backhanded the ball, leaped in the air, and fired a bullet to first base.

It was a close play, but the runner beat the ball by a split second. The umpire yelled "Safe," while at the same time he raised his clenched fist and thumb in the air to signal "out."

"Well, which is it, am I safe or out?" the bewildered base runner demanded.

The umpire replied, "You know you're safe and I know you're safe. But 30,000 people think you're out, so you're out!"

I'm not even going to tell you about the rhubarb that followed. It is interesting to note, though, that it really doesn't matter what reality is, it's what people perceive to be reality that counts.

THE BIGGER THEY ARE

I've met a lot of tall and big people who are wonderfully kind and considerate and who go out of their way to make certain they don't intimidate others with their superior, physical size.

On the other hand, I've met some tall and big people who definitely use their size to try to intimidate and bully others. I've even heard of tall people who've sawed an inch or two off the legs of the visitor's chairs in their office to make certain visitors would feel small and inferior.

And I've noticed lots of these big guys like to stand toe to toe with a smaller person so they can look straight down at them in an attempt to make them wilt.

I must admit, when I conceived the idea for this book on how to get what you want through finesse, tact, creativity, and strategy instead of force and intimidation, I had a couple of these huge bozos in mind.

So, if you're dealing with a person of large physical size who uses that size to intimidate and bully, how do you hold your own?

Well, first of all, realize that the reason a lot of these big guys rely on their superior, physical size to intimidate is that it's their greatest strength. Sometimes, they don't have a lot of knowledge, substance, facts, or creativity to carry them.

So, how do you deal with these intimidating bullies on equal, or even superior, ground?

Actually, the solution is quite simple. Don't deal with them face-to-face. You can totally neutralize their superior, physical size by dealing with them over the telephone. Or, you can use the mail, fax, or e-mail. When they can't see you and tower over you, they must deal with you totally by using their intellect, creativity, and knowledge. And, when it comes down to that, I've seen some of these big intimidators reduced to pussycats.

Just for fun, sometime, when you're talking to one of these big guys over the phone, you might want to stand on your chair or on your desk so you can turn the tables on them and experience the exhilaration that comes from being ten feet tall and bulletproof. Go ahead — they deserve it.

PLEASE RETURN MY CALL

Doesn't it just irritate the heck out of you when you leave a message for someone to return your phone call, and they never call you back.

Why don't they? Well, maybe they forgot, or they were too busy. Or, to be honest, maybe they don't view you or your topic of conversation interesting enough or important enough to return the call.

But you really need to talk to them. So, how are you going to entice them to return your call?

Well, my friend, Nancy, tells me about her friend, Herman, who's devised a sure-fire system to get virtually anyone to return his calls. And, it's fun, helps lighten up the day, and puts the caller in a positive frame of mind to boot — usually.

And, here it is. When Herman calls someone who's not in, he always leaves a message. A message like, "I have proof that man had sex with the buffalo at least 3,000 years ago. Call me for details. Herman." Or, "The alignment of the stars in relationship to the moon indicates that tomorrow will be a fantastic day to achieve great wealth in (a few garbled words of gobbley gook, here). It is imperative that I talk to you today before 4:00 P.M. Herman."

Well, you get the idea. Humorous or outrageous or leading statements or questions that compel the recipient to pick up the phone and call you. If you work at it, you can have a lot of fun with this — anybody can do it. For instance, here's one that I just came up with. "Hi, this is Peter Davidson. Is it true that your (a few words of gobbley gook here) is pregnant?"

It's probably a good idea to only use this technique over the phone. In closer quarters it might get you socked in the eye.

SURPRISE PACKAGE

The strike had gone on for nine days, and just about everyone in the city was starting to fear they'd be buried alive.

It wouldn't have been so bad if the strikers had been the city hall employees or public librarians or police officers or fire fighters, but it was more serious than that. The workers on strike were the city garbage collectors, and the garbage was beginning to pile up in closets, hallways, and porches. Everywhere you looked, in alleys, street corners, and boulevards, there were piles of garbage.

Everyone grumbled about the mountains of garbage, and just about everyone resigned themselves to the fact that they'd have to just keep piling it up until the strike was over. Everyone, that is, but Josh Hendricks.

Josh didn't want to be surrounded with the mess, odor, and unsightliness of piles of garbage stacked around his home, and he decided to do something about it. And he became one of the few people in the entire city that didn't spend half of their day moaning and groaning about the garbage strike. In fact, Josh enjoyed the strike.

Josh simply came up with a creative way to solve his garbage problem. Each day he boxed up his garbage and wrapped the box in colorful, wrapping paper and put a bow on the box. Then, he put the box in the back seat of his car, parked his car along a busy street, and left the door unlocked. Each day when he returned to his car after work, the box was gone.

Josh had only two regrets over his garbage disposal project. One was that he wished he'd have been there to see the look on the thief's face when they opened the package, and the other was that the strike lasted for only twelve days.

IV.
WHEELIN' 'N' DEALIN'

Every week you're involved in dozens of negotiations. Most of them are small potatoes, like trying to decide with family members what to have for dinner, deciding who's going to wash dishes, trying to convince someone to give you a ride downtown, trying to get someone to run a few errands for you, or trying to get your kids or spouse to do what you want.

Once in a while, though, the negotiations are for higher stakes — like when buying a house, taking a new job, or buying a car.

You can go into these negotiations unprepared and get waxed, or you can plan in advance and have the upper hand. The latter sounds better.

> *If you must play, decide on three things at the start: the rules of the game, the stakes, and the quitting time.* Chinese proverb

> *When you want to test the depths of a stream, don't use both feet.* Chinese proverb

> *Being powerful is like being a lady. If you have to tell people you are, you aren't.* Margaret Thatcher

> *If you reveal your secrets to the wind, you should not blame the wind for revealing them to the trees.* Khalil Gibran

> *Don't play for safety — it's the most dangerous thing in the world.* Hugh Walpole

We go by the major vote, and if the majority are insane, the sane must go to the hospital. Horace Mann

Trust everybody, but cut the cards. Finley Peter Dunne

Keep your broken arm inside your sleeve. Chinese proverb

The fellow who agrees with everything you say is either a fool or he is getting ready to skin you. Kin Hubbard

Beware of the young doctor and the old barber. Benjamin Franklin

People will buy anything that is one to the customer. Sinclair Lewis

Don't ask a barber whether you need a haircut. Daniel Greenberg

Call on God, but row away from the rocks. Indian proverb

An army of sheep led by a lion would defeat an army of lions led by a sheep. Arab proverb

AFTER YOU

My friend, Ron, is a Certified Public Accountant. This story didn't actually happen to Ron personally, but it happened to one of his CPA colleagues, Charles, a few years back. And, Ron told me about it.

Charles had prepared the year-end financial statements and tax returns for a small manufacturer in his community for many years. The owner, Nels, decided to sell the company. He ran an ad in a trade journal and soon got an inquiry from another manufacturer located some 200 miles to the north. Through a series of phone calls and mailings, information, including income and expenses, was exchanged. The prospective buyer visited the man-ufacturing plant and went home to ponder the possibility of mak-ing an offer.

Soon, the call came. The prospective buyer wanted to make an offer. It was decided that Nels, accompanied by his long-time accountant, Charles, would drive to the prospective buyer's office for a meeting.

As they made the 200-mile journey, Nels and Charles had plen-ty of time to discuss the strategy. Nels said, simply, if they didn't offer him two million dollars he wouldn't sell. Two million dollars — that was his price. Final. Firm. Kapoot. That was it. Not one cent less.

After a few pleasantries were exchanged, the meeting got down to brass tacks.

"We are prepared to make you an offer," the prospective buyer began.

Nels took a deep breath and braced himself for it. "They'll try to steal it." "This was a waste of time." "I should get up and leave right now rather than sit here and be embarrassed by their puny offer." "They're a bunch of cheapskates — you can tell just by looking at them." "Dammit, nobody's gonna steal my business." The thoughts rushed through Nel's head.

The prospective buyer smiled, looked Nels square in the eye and said, "We'll offer you three million dollars — cash."

The offer hit Nels like a sledgehammer. He could feel the blood rush to his head as his heart started to pound wildly. He broke out in an instant sweat and felt cold and clammy all at the same time. He could feel his eyes start to roll, and he gasped for air. In fear of throwing up on the table or of passing out in front of everyone, he struggled to his feet and staggered out the door. Charles helped Nels to a chair in the outer foyer and returned to the meeting.

"Gentlemen," Charles began in a firm, if not condescending tone, "As you can see, your offer made my client physically ill. If you want to buy his company, you'll have to get serious."

And, they did get serious. They offered four million dollars, which Charles begrudgingly accepted on behalf of his client, Nels.

It's a good thing Nels was out in the foyer when Charles turned down the three million dollar offer, or Nels probably would have had the big one right on the spot.

In another similar negotiation, my old college roommate, Galen, once sold a business for $750,000 more than he expected, simply because he let the buyer talk first.

In still another situation, a friend told me that he found out his teenage son, Brad's, girlfriend was pregnant. He agonized over the situation all day long. Should he confront his son? Should he talk to the girl? Should he call the girl's parents? He felt miserable.

When he got home from work, he felt even worse — there was a message for him to call the girl's father. No doubt, the girl's father would lambaste him for being a poor example and a miserable father and would attack his son for being a dirty, rotten, low-down, miserable scumbag.

Finally, the man worked up the courage to call the girl's father. As the phone rang, he rehearsed, one last time, the words he would use to express his disappointment in his son and how he would vow to help out in any way he could.

The girl's father picked up the phone on the other end, but before the boy's father could begin his speech, the girl's father began to talk.

"I've been trying to reach Brad all day," the girl's father began, "but I haven't been able to find him. I need Brad to help me carry an old couch down to the basement. Please ask him to stop by sometime tonight. Thanks. Good-bye."

Brad's father heaved a sigh of relief as he hung up the phone. Apparently, the girl's father didn't know she was pregnant; but, it would only postpone the lambasting that was sure to come when he did find out.

Well, that was a couple of years ago. As it turned out, the girl never was pregnant — it was some other Brad and his girlfriend that the rumor was about.

Even today, Brad's father goes limp when he recalls the story and imagines the mess he'd have made if he would have blurted out his confession and apology to the girl's father.

Life is full of situations like these three examples where you might have the option of speaking first or of letting the other person do the honors. As you can see, it's often to your advantage to display some real manners here and to simply say, "After you."

THE AMERICAN DREAM

I'm a real estate broker. My license is active, but I'm not. Haven't been since I started writing books like this one. But I once was active, and I was involved in the listing and sale of millions of dollars of property. And I've taught real estate courses and have written a couple of books on the subject, so I've come to fancy myself as being somewhat knowledgeable on the topic.

It is still the American Dream — to own a home. And, the majority of Americans will live this dream in their lifetime. Many will buy and sell several homes as family status, finances, and lifestyles change.

Buying a home is a science and an art. The science part amounts to properly analyzing your needs and finances to identify a home that is suitable and to then actually locate that home. The art part amounts to using proper negotiating techniques to get that home bought at the lowest possible price. This story is about the art part.

Place yourself in this situation, and see how you would handle it. You want to buy a home. You know exactly what size, style, and price of home you want. Finally, after much searching, you find that home. It is listed for sale at $145,000, which is a fair price — maybe a little high. You, of course, want to buy the home at as low a price as you can. Realize, too, that the owner wants to sell the home at as high a price as they can.

You determine that you will offer $135,000 for the home. You came up with this price based on the feeling that the seller should come down a little, as a normal negotiating procedure, and because the house is not in perfect condition and needs a little work. Precisely, you think it will cost $6,000 to make the required improvements and that the seller should drop the price $4,000 simply because they should negotiate a little. And $135,000 is stretching your finances about as far as they will go.

Let's say you are dealing face-to-face with the owner and are about to present your $135,000 offer. You realize this is asking the owner to take $10,000 less than they want. Your task is to artfully convince the seller that they should take your offer. Here are two options of what you might say to the owner:

> *Option A*: "Mr. and Mrs. Seller, my spouse and I would like to make an offer of $135,000 on your home. We realize this is $10,000 less than you are

asking, but let me explain how I came up with the $135,000 figure.

"While this is a fine home, there are a few things that will need to be done to restore it to its original condition. I've made a list. There are two cracked windowpanes that will need to be replaced. The windowsills in most rooms will need to be refinished, and some may need to be replaced. There are some scratches and scars in the woodwork and kitchen cabinets, and they will need to be sanded and varnished. The carpeting in the family room and living room has received a lot of use, and we'd like to replace it. Also, some of the walls have smudges on them, and we'll want to paint most of the rooms. Another item is the furnace — it looks pretty old and will probably need to be replaced soon. There are a few other items on my list, but they're pretty minor. Anyway, I hope you can understand why we're offering $135,000 and hope you can accept it."

Option B: "Mr. and Mrs. Seller, my spouse and I would like to make an offer of $135,000 on your home. I realize this is $10,000 less than you are asking, but it is all we can afford to pay.

"We fell in love with your home, and we are excited about the possibility of living here. We particularly like the large kitchen-dining area, and all the rooms seem to flow together so well. And we really like the family room — it's so cozy. We've told the kids all about the house, and they're excited about it. Oh, we may make a few changes here and there, but basically we love the house as it is. We really hope you can accept our offer."

Well, which procedure would you use — Option A or Option B? Go ahead, make a selection.

Now let's analyze each approach. The philosophy in Option A is to justify the lower price with the use of logic. The house needs some work that will cost the buyer money, which is why the lower price is being offered. The hope is that the seller will admit that these logical statements are true and that the lower price of $135,000 is therefore justified.

The philosophy in Option B is to appeal to the seller's emotions instead of their logic. The buyer says, "This is a great home. We love it. You can entrust your home to us and have peace of mind knowing that it will be well cared for and appreciated."

So, what is the most effective approach? Well, Option A is the *sledgehammer approach*. You are trying to beat down the price by saying negative things about the home. In effect, what you are saying is, "This place is a pit, but I'd like to buy it, anyway, and see if I can fix it up."

Option B uses *finesse*. You are trying to entice the seller to *want* to sell to you, because you love the home, as they do, and they can entrust its care to you.

Keep in mind that this is more than a house to the seller. It is a *home*. It is the place the children came home to from the hospital when they were born. It is the place where tears were shed, scratches were bandaged, and little broken hearts were mended. It is the place where birthdays, graduations, anniversaries, and other triumphs were celebrated. To the seller it has been stability, belonging, pride, and roots.

I have watched buyers use these two approaches many times. When confronted with an Option A (sledgehammer) buyer, I've heard more than one seller say, "We wouldn't sell our home to that S.O.B. no matter how much he offered."

On the other hand, a seller *likes* the buyer who uses Option B (finesse) and *wants* to see them live in their home. It doesn't mean that a buyer using this approach always gets their offer accepted or that they always get the property bought. If the offer is too low, well, the seller just can't accept it no matter how much they like the potential buyer.

But, I have heard a number of sellers say, "We like those people. We'd feel good about having them living in our home. The offer isn't as high as we'd like, but we'll take it."

In effect, sellers seem to say this to buyers: "It isn't perfect, we know that, but damned be the person who comes in here and ridicules it. We'll sell our *home* to someone who will appreciate it, love it, and care for it."

When you purchase your next home, you may want to offer less than the asking price. You can use either the sledgehammer approach or finesse. You may find that using finesse will save you several hundred times the price you paid for this book. And that you end up getting the home you want.

RED HERRINGS

In the typical murder mystery, there are normally four, five, or six suspects, each of whom could easily be the murderer. Each has motive and opportunity. Each may have actually wanted the deceased dead. Each of them probably had some confrontation with the deceased where they threatened to kill them. Or each of them stood to gain a great deal by that person being dead. Of course, only one of the suspects is the guilty party. The rest are just inserted into the story to throw us off, which is called *misdirection*. The innocent suspects are also referred to as *red herrings* or *straw men*.

Maybe you're not going to write a murder mystery, but you can utilize the principle of *misdirection* in many of your daily business or personal activities. For instance, when involved in any negotiation, you can plant a few red herrings or straw men, also called *bargaining chips*. That is, you can ask for things that you don't really want and that you can eventually give up to make it look like you're really trying hard to compromise. But, since you didn't really want those red herrings in the first place, you're actually giving up nothing.

Employer-employee negotiating teams know all about red herrings. Say for instance, that the employer and the employees are negotiating salaries and other terms for next year's contract. And, let's further say that all similar companies that have recently settled ended up with a five percent pay raise.

So, what do the employer and the employees make as their initial bargaining offers? Well, the employer offers a raise of 0 percent (red herring). Further, the employer now wants employees to work nights (red herring) and weekends (red herring), to pay all of their own insurance costs (red herring), and to work all holidays (red herring).

The employees want a twenty percent pay raise (red herring) want to decrease the work week to thirty hours (red herring), want fifteen more vacation days per year (red herring), and want the employer to contribute $10,000 per year into a pension plan for each employee (red herring).

When the dust settles, the employer and employees will probably agree on a five percent pay raise, like everybody else got, and the other bargaining items, red herrings all, will be forgotten about.

You can use red herrings in your personal life, too. Say you're negotiating with an auto dealer for the purchase of a new car. You tell the dealer that what you want is leather seats (red herring — cloth or vinyl would be fine), a sunroof (red herring — you hate them), seven-way power seats (red herring — regular seats would be fine), and chrome wheels (red herring — regular wheel covers would be fine). When the dealer can't deliver a car with all of your required features, you now attempt to negotiate downward in price from the dealer's initial price since they can't deliver the car you say you want.

Or, how about the sweet young thing who wants her father to give her money to buy a new dress. She starts out by telling her father she needs money to buy new shoes, a coat, a necklace, a blouse, and slacks. By the time, it's over, her father is begging to buy her a dress, if she'll just forget about the rest of the stuff.

Or, you're making an offer on a house. Your offer states the following are to stay with the house: curtains and drapes (these, you really want), the door bell that plays a tune (red herring), the stove and refrigerator (these you need), the washer and dryer (red herring), the dining room chandelier (you want this), and the piano in the basement (red herring). That should be plenty of red herrings to give you a little bargaining room.

Our list of examples could go on and on, and you can probably add some situations of your own where you've thrown in a red herring or two.

The neat thing about red herrings is that you know where the red herrings are, but nobody else does. The bad thing, however, is that the party you're negotiating with probably has a whole bunch of red herrings all over the place, too. But, what the heck, we'll have a lot of fun with all these red herrings, before it's all over.

WE'LL GIVE 'IM A FAIR TRIAL,
AND THEN WE'LL HANG THE GUILTY S.O.B.

I was teaching a college business law class. About half the students in the class were from the law program, and the other half were business students. An interesting mixture.

My favorite part of the course was the cases for discussion at the end of each chapter. Here, we looked at applying the facts and procedures that had been presented in the reading material.

My favorite case in the whole book was a simple one, but it presented the opportunity for a wide range of potential solutions ranging from using a feather to using a ten-pound sledgehammer.

Here's the case: "A young couple got married and hired a professional photographer to take wedding pictures. Upon returning from their honeymoon, they noticed that the photographer was displaying a large portrait of their wedding in his photography shop window. The bride and groom were very upset. They viewed their wedding as a private affair, not to be shared with the general public and not to be commercialized. What should the bride and groom do?"

After reading the case aloud in class, I instructed the students to jot down their solution before we discussed the case. So, I'll ask you to do the same thing. What would you advise the bride and groom to do? Write down your solution.

After giving the students a little time, but not too much, I asked, "Well, what should the bride and groom do?"

"Sue 'em," shouted several law students.

"Get an injunction," yelled another.

"Take 'em to court," said a couple more.

I *knew* that was what the law students would say. They *always* said that, every semester for the past five years. It is the mind-set of a lawyer. The students were being shaped and molded nicely for their profession.

Then, I would call on a business student, "What would you advise the bride and groom to do?"

Invariably, the business student would say, "Well, I think they should go talk to the photographer and ask him to remove the photograph."

I always enjoyed watching the law students' reaction to that possible solution. Their faces seemed to say, "Hmmm. Never thought of that. Might work."

I then enjoyed describing to the class, a little tongue-in-cheek, that the first solution law students always thought of for any confrontation was to "sue 'em," but that business students had been trained to first seek an amiable solution before bringing out the heavy artillery. Even the law students smiled.

Then we made a list of the options available to solve the bride and groom's problem and ranked them in the sequence that should be applied. It is important to recognize what the problem really is and what the perturbed party wants to have done to make things right. In this case, the problem was the photograph was being displayed in public. The solution sought by the perturbed party, the bride and groom, was to have the photograph removed. Following is our list of potential solutions, ranked in the order they should be applied, to solve the bride and groom's problem.

Step 1 — Approach the photographer pleasantly, explain that you want your wedding photos to be private, and ask him to remove the photo from the window. Most likely, the photographer will apologize sincerely and will remove the photograph immediately. Chances are the photographer will give you the photograph from the window as a goodwill offering. And, you will forgive the photographer completely, think highly of him, and do business with him for many years to come. Here, both the bride and groom and the photographer handled the situation with finesse.

Step 2 — If the photographer refuses to remove the photograph from the window, you now have confrontation, and it was caused by the photographer. A sharp letter from your attorney will probably get the photographer's attention and will get the photograph removed from the window.

Step 3 — If the photographer unwisely ignores the attorney's letter, now is the time to "Sue 'em," "Get an injunction," "Take 'em to court."

Yes, there are several potential solutions to a problem, ranging from the "feather approach" to the sledgehammer. And, often the problem can be solved cordially, without creating hard feelings. But, if finesse doesn't work, you can always bring out the sledgehammer, later.

THE LOYALTY OATH

Here's what happened to my friend, Ron, a real estate salesman.

Ron got the name of a couple who were moving to town, called them, and set up an appointment to show them houses the next weekend. He got along fabulously with the couple, but they didn't find a house that seemed right. So they made an appointment to look at additional houses the next weekend. For four consecutive weekends, they looked at houses. Finally, late Saturday afternoon, they found a house they wanted to buy. But they wanted to "sleep on it," before they took the big leap. Ron made an appointment to meet them at his office on Sunday morning at 10:00 to write up the offer.

At 10:05 A.M., Ron's office phone rang. It was his house buyers.

"You're going to be so happy for us," the voice said, "we found a house we just love and bought it last night."

Happy for them? Ron would have choked them if he could have gotten his hands on them.

But Ron kept his cool. He assured them that he was, indeed, happy for them and that there were no hard feelings. As it turned out, a stranger at the next table had struck up a conversation with them during dinner on Saturday night. The stranger was a real estate agent who convinced them to look at a house he'd just listed. They fell in love with it and bought it on the spot.

Ron hung up the phone and was so upset that he could hardly see straight. This wasn't the first time that something like this had happened to Ron, and he knew it happened to virtually every real estate agent once in awhile. But none of that helped relieve the disappointment and the anger. Whatever happened to loyalty? Ron had devoted four weekends to these people, and they bought from someone else.

Loyalty. Ron thought about that for a few moments — LOYALTY. What could he do to increase his customer's loyalty — to get them to stick with him until the end?

And then it hit him. The customers weren't at all concerned about being loyal to him. They were concerned about themselves and their own wants and needs. And when you come down to it, the customer probably should pursue every possibility open to them to find the best deal they can.

And then it really hit Ron. The reason these people had bought from someone else is that he had failed in his loyalty to them — had failed by not finding the right home for them to buy.

So, Ron created *The Loyalty Oath*. He prepared a written statement identifying what he would do to be loyal to his customers: (1) He would put the customer's interests first, ahead of his own; (2) He would show them every house on the market, including those listed for sale by other real estate agents; (3) He would work with them as long as it took to find a home they wanted to buy; (4) Etc.; (5) Etc.; (6) Etc.

Ron reads the loyalty oath to his customers, making quite a production of it, signs it, and gives it to them.

In return Ron asks one thing of his customers — their loyalty. Specifically, he tells them this: (1) If you see a home advertised in the newspaper or see a lawn sign on a house you want to see, tell me about it, and I'll make arrangements to show it to you; (2) If another real estate agent calls you and wants to show you property, tell them you're working with me; (3) If another real estate agent tells you that they have a new listing that I'm not aware of, tell them I'll contact them to make arrangements to show it to you; (4) Etc.; (5) Etc.; (6) Etc.

And Ron fulfills his pledge of loyalty unfailingly. And his customers have, in turn, become much more loyal to him — all because Ron finally figured out who owed what degree of loyalty to whom. After that, if was easy.

EASY MONEY

This little ditty will earn you 50-100 times the cost of this book every year for the rest of your life if you apply its principle correctly. Even if you apply the principle halfway correctly, it will earn you 10-20 times the cost of this book every year for the rest of your life. But, first of all, a little background.

I'll admit that when I was a youth I was sometimes embarrassed by my dad. The reason I was embarrassed was that sometimes he was so tight — bordering on being cheap.

I recall, for instance, when my mom and dad and I went shopping for a new suit for me to wear to my junior prom. The price tag on the outfit was $50. (This was several decades ago, you know.) It fit good and looked great, and I really wanted it. But, instead of just going ahead and buying it like anybody else would, my dad looked that clothing store guy in the eye and said, "I'll give you $45 for it." I could have died from the embarrassment.

The clothing store guy looked a little shocked — I doubt many buyers haggled over the price of a suit. But he took one good look at my dad and saw he meant business, so he took the $45.

And, this wasn't the only time my dad haggled over the price of things he bought. I remember him doing the same thing when buying cars, equipment, tires, jewelry, furniture, and just about anything that cost over $50. And, boy, was I embarrassed every time that he did it.

Well, that was a long time ago, and I've learned a lot since then. I learned, for instance, that my dad wasn't tight or cheap at all — he was smart. That $5 he saved on my prom suit — that was in an era where $1 an hour was considered to be a good wage. My dad made almost a day's pay, after taxes, just by asking for it.

So, there's the secret on how to make the easiest money you'll ever earn in your life — ASK FOR IT.

Some people are reluctant to ask for a discount or to haggle on the price, because they feel it is demeaning or that it makes them look cheap.

Maybe this will help. Legally, in almost all cases, the price shown in an advertisement or catalog, the price shown on goods in a store window, and the price shown on the price tag attached to goods are considered to be "invitations for the buyer to negotiate." They are normally *not* considered to be offers to sell at those prices. It is the *buyer* who makes the offer to buy at a certain price.

Usually the buyer offers the price shown on the price tag, and the seller accepts it — but there is no reason you can't offer less than the sticker price.

If you're one of those people who feel uncomfortable haggling over price or asking the seller to take less, here are a few simple-to-use, non-threatening statements that may help.

"Can you do any better than that on price?"

"Sharpen your pencil, and see what price you can come up with."

"What's your best price on that?"

"If I were to buy three of them, what price can you give me?"

Often, this is all that it takes to get the ball rolling. And, if the seller won't lower their price, you can always pay the sticker price or go buy it elsewhere.

So, next time you buy something that has a fairly large price tag, go ahead and ask for a better deal. You'll be surprised at how many merchants will quickly grab their calculator, and it will be the easiest money you'll ever make in your life. Guaranteed.

HAVE A CHAIR

You have an important meeting with a business executive where you will attempt to sell him $50,000 of your goods. You enter his office and notice a large, uncluttered desk with the executive's high-backed chair behind it. Across from the desk are two padded chairs for visitors. Off to the side of the office is a table with six matching chairs around it.

You have a number of books, charts, and materials to spread out and show to the executive. Your presentation can be made equally well at the executive's desk, with the executive behind the desk and you sitting in a visitor's chair, or at the table off to the side of the room.

Regardless of where you sit, you know there's going to be some negotiation of price and terms, and you'll have to be at your best to hold your own.

You know you can make the presentation equally well at the executive's desk or at the table, but the executive doesn't know this. Thus, with a little logic and an explanation, you can probably direct the executive to either site for the presentation.

So where do you want to make your presentation, at the desk or at the table? Question two — why?

One of your goals in making the presentation is to be on as equal grounds as you can with your client — your adversary. Being in his office, with familiar surroundings for him and foreign surroundings for you, is bad enough. Let's not give the client an additional advantage by choosing the wrong seating arrangement.

Hopefully, you looked the client's office over, noting the uncluttered desk and the table with chairs and said something like this: "I have so many things to spread out and to show you, I think the table will work best."

And, hopefully you headed in that direction before the executive could raise an objection.

You see, when someone sits behind their desk, they have a cannon in front of them. Whose territory is this — the person behind the desk or the person sitting in the visitor's chair? Who's in charge here — the person behind the desk or the one in the visitor's chair? Well, you see what I mean.

Moving your client out from behind his desk to the table will put the two of you on more equal grounds. But, we're not finished yet.

Let's say the client is the same sex as you. Let's also assume that you can maneuver the client to sit at the table wherever you want. So, will you direct the client to sit across from you or next to you? I'm serious — what would you do?

Well, studies show this: Sitting across the table from someone of the same sex creates a confrontational situation; sitting beside them creates trust. Sitting across the table from someone of the opposite sex creates trust; sitting beside them creates confrontation.

So, here's another quiz. If you're going to meet with a man and a woman, where in relation to them should you sit at the table?

Answer: Based on the previous information, you should position yourself to sit next to the person of your same sex and across the table from the person of the opposite sex.

While we're talking about choosing sites for a meeting, let's go back to the beginning.

If possible, always have the meeting at your office. Here you can be the powerful one sitting behind your cannon of a desk. If that doesn't work, settle for a neutral site. That's why business lunches are so popular — a neutral playing field.

But, if all else fails and you must meet your client at his or her office, try your best to get them out from behind that cannon that they've got aimed at you. Boom.

THE INVISIBLE STORE

Harold and Clara ran a Ma and Pa variety and department store on main street. The store didn't make them rich, but they made a good living.

They had lived in fear for years of a circumstance that they thought they couldn't avoid. And when the circumstance hit them; it hit them with a double whammy.

Not only was one national chain store coming to town, but two of them were. And, worse than that, one of them was going to locate on each side of their store, with Harold and Clara's Variety squashed in-between.

The two chain stores opened on the same weekend to much hoopla and fanfare. Their fancy storefronts and big signs seemed to pull customers like a magnet. Customers rushed from one chain store to another without even noticing Harold and Clara's little store stuck in between.

In the weeks and months to come, customers rushed to the two chain stores and Harold and Clara's variety remained all but invisible. Business dropped off dramatically, and it looked like the little variety store was doomed unless some miracle happened.

The miracle happened one night when an idea popped into Harold's head. The next day he withdrew a precious $200 from the store's account in a last-ditch attempt to save the store.

And the $200 idea worked wonders. Now, virtually everyone who heads to the two chain stores to shop stops at Harold and Clara's Variety first, and, with the superior service and advice that Harold and Clara give, they sell a lot of stuff.

The miracle that turned it all around was a two word sign that Harold had painted in huge letters and that he hung above the front door to Harold and Clara's Variety.

The sign said: Main Entrance.

THE GOLDEN RULE

I was sitting at the lunch counter in a small cafe when a man walked in, spotted the guy sitting a couple of stools down from me, and walked up to him.

The man on the stool saw him coming in the mirror and turned to greet him.

"Hi, Ralph," he said with a smile, "That new faucet and sink I put in for you still working?"

"Yeah, the damn thing works," he replied in a tone that was somewhere between mean and mad.

"I don't know who the hell you plumbers think you are — doctors or something — charging like that. Three hundred and sixty dollars is just too damn much for a little job like that," he continued.

"Well, I'm sorry you feel that way, Ralph," the plumber began, "But all the old pipes were rusted and needed to be replaced, and some of the old fittings were so old they didn't match the new plumbing and had to be replaced — it was all listed on the bill. In fact, I didn't even charge you for a few spare parts I had on hand that I used."

"You saw a chance to rip me off, and you took it," Ralph said. "You plumbers and carpenters and mechanics and electricians are all the same — ripping people off."

"I'm sorry you feel that way, but the bill really was legitimate — not padded," the plumber said, trying to gently handle the man's anger.

"I'll tell you one thing," Ralph said, "You'll never work for me again."

"Tell me something," the plumber, said, "Did you pay the bill?"

"Yeah, I paid your damn bill," Ralph sneered.

The plumber stood up, looked Ralph straight in the eye and said, "Then screw you," and he walked out.

I smiled inwardly and said to myself, "The Golden Rule still works — he who has the gold, rules."

DOOR KNOB 'EM

When you get in a debate, discussion, or argument, the doorknob might be your best friend. Professional salespeople all know this and use the doorknob shamelessly. Let me explain.

Say a salesperson is sitting at your kitchen table, trying to convince you to buy life insurance. They've given you their entire canned presentation, complete with flip charts, tables, graphs, and computer printouts. They've tried to close the sale seven times, but you've fought back their every attempt. It's been a tense, stressful session.

Finally, the insurance salesperson packs up their gear and, while doing so, shifts the conversation to a more light-hearted topic — off of insurance, finally. It appears they're surrendering. You've won. What a relief. For the first time in an hour you can start to relax.

The insurance salesperson packs up their gear, stands up, and heads slowly for the door to leave, carrying on a pleasant conversation all the while.

They approach the door and reach for the doorknob. In five seconds they'll be gone. What a relief. What a triumph.

They grab the doorknob and then, all of a sudden, they let go of it and snap their fingers as a new flash of inspiration hits them.

"Oh," they say, "I forgot to tell you about a very important feature of this program."

Next thing you know, you're sitting back at the table, and they're blazing away again.

The door knob technique, with the new flash of inspiration, was no accident. It's all a carefully planned technique, used to relax difficult-to-sell prospects, to throw them off guard, and to take another shot at making the sale.

You can use this same technique when involved in debates, discussions, and arguments in your personal life. Just one word of caution. Don't let the doorknob hit you in the, um, posterior, on the way out the door.

WORLD'S TOP BROOM SELLER

Glenn ran a small, neighborhood, grocery store — a Ma and Pa operation — in a small, resort community and sold more brooms than any other store of any size in the world.

So, were the local residents on a cleanliness kick? Not necessarily. Did they wear out their brooms sweeping the sidewalk and the street? Nope. Were they eating the brooms or burning them in their fireplaces? Nope, and, nope, again. In truth, the residents didn't use their brooms more frequently or for any more unusual purposes than anyone else. But almost everybody who shopped in Glenn's store bought a broom.

So, why did they buy so many brooms, and what did they do with them? Well, let me explain.

Glenn ran the cash register himself. As he rang up each sale, he would state the item purchased and say its price. Let's listen in.

"Good morning — eggs, $1.45; hamburger, $2.48; lemonade, $1.98, and a broom, $4.50."

Next customer: "Good morning — bacon, $3.76; bread, $1.29; milk, $1.97; and a broom, $4.50."

Next customer: "Good morning — tomatoes, $1.58; potatoes, $2.49; milk, $1.97; and a broom, $4.50."

You see, Glenn had hit upon a clever sales tactic. Each morning he strategically placed a brand new broom at the end of the checkout counter. And, as he rang up each item on the cash register, he pushed it past himself down to the end of the counter — to where the broom was sitting. And, of course, since there was a broom down there by the rest of the stuff they were buying, Glen just "assumed" that they were buying the broom, also. Of course, since the customer hadn't planned on buying a broom, they assumed it belonged to someone else, and they just left it sitting there. And then Glenn sold it to the next customer, and the next, and the next.

Okay — so Glenn was a crook. But, he was a clever crook.

Or some would say Glenn just used the "assumption close" practiced by many salespeople — that he used the assumption close to the max. With this technique, you assume that the customer's going to buy, so you go ahead and ring up the sale, write up the sales ticket, start wrapping up the item, or do something else that indicates you assume the buyer is going to buy. And, if the customer doesn't want to buy, they've got to step in and stop you. Maybe Glenn wasn't a crook after all — maybe he was just applying the good old assumption close. Ha.

But anyway, I thought you'd enjoy seeing how the top broom salesman in the world did it.

And, I've got an assignment for you. See if you can develop some type of legal and ethical application for Glenn's technique. If you can, you'll be so rich; you'll be able to buy yourself anything you want, and a broom.

THE FORTY HOUR MYTH

Okay, its time for a quiz. There are only three questions and each will take from five seconds to thirty seconds to read and about ten seconds to answer. So, the whole quiz will take less than two minutes. But, play along with me, will you, and write down your answers on a sheet of scratch paper. Or, at least, firmly fix an answer to each in your mind. Here are the questions:

1. How many hours per week does the successful business executive work?

2. How many hours per week does the self-made millionaire, who is still active in their endeavors, work?

3. You are a college student. There will be only three exams in a course you are taking, and your final grade will be calculated as an average of those three exams. Your first exam will be in four days, and it covers six chapters — that's 200 pages of textbook material. You have already read the six chapters that the test will cover. How many hours will you study for the exam?

Got your answers written down?

There isn't one specific answer to any of the three questions, but there is a range of acceptable answers, as described below:

1. The number of hours worked per week by successful business executives ranges from about 50-90, with 60-70 being common.

2. The number of hours worked per week by the successful, self-made millionaire who is still active in his or her affairs is similar to those worked by the successful executive, with 60-80 being common.

3. The number of hours you would study for the upcoming major exam could vary widely, depending upon the grade you will be satisfied with and how much you have studied already.

But, let's assume that you've merely read the six chapters so far and haven't gotten down to any hard-core studying until now. And, you don't even have to take the test to get your grade — I'll assign it to you based on the amount of time you studied. Ask any teacher, they'll tell you that the following grading scale is pretty accurate. Study time of 0-1 hours = F; 2-4 hours = D; 5-7 hours = C; 8-10 hours = B; 11-12 hours = A-; 13 hours or more = A.

The three parties identified in our little three-question quiz, the business executive, the self-made millionaire, and the college student, will need to apply a combination of skills, abilities, and factors to be truly successful. But one of the most important of these is *time*.

In our society, we have come to think of the forty hour work-week as the standard. It's the number of hours most people work and most people prefer to work no more than that. And there's nothing wrong with that. The truth is, you can earn a living working forty hours a week — often a very good living.

But, if you aspire to achieve extraordinary things in life, the forty hour workweek is a myth. Ask any successful business executive, self-made millionaire, or other person who has accomplished great things, and they'll tell you the same thing — forty hours is only a warm-up. It simply is not enough time to do all that must be done.

If a person works forty hours a week, has two weeks' vacation per year and gets five holidays off, they actually work forty-nine weeks in a year. At forty hours per week, that's 1,960 hours (49 x 40 = 1,960) worked in a year.

On the other hand, if a person has the same vacation schedule but works seventy hours a week, they will work 3,430 hours (70 x 49 = 3,430) in a year. In a year's time, this person will work 1,470 hours more than the person working the standard forty hour week. In ten years, they will have worked the equivalent of seventeen and one half years and in a forty year career, they will have worked the equivalent of seventy years. That's thirty additional years in which to accomplish their goals and to do things!

So, where do these human dynamos get the time to work all those extra hours? First of all, they don't have more hours available to them in a week that anyone else — just the standard 168 hour week. Second, contrary to popular belief, they are not necessarily "workaholics" who do nothing but work, eat, sleep, and work. Many of these people have as active social and recreational lives as those who work forty hours a week. So, where do they get the time? Let's look at a few examples.

Mark is a successful business executive who works at least seventy hours a week. Whereas the average American adult watches more than twenty-six hours of television per week, Mark watches very little. There's most of his extra time.

Paula packs a "brown bag" lunch every day. Instead of taking an hour or hour-and-a-half lunch break at a restaurant like her colleagues, Paula enjoys a leisurely lunch in her office while she catches up on reading company reports. That gives her five to seven and one half hours of extra work time per week, or about seven extra weeks a year.

Gary commutes from his suburban home to his job in the city. He avoids wasting time getting stuck in rush-hour traffic by leaving home a half hour earlier than most commuters and by returning home a half hour later than most. And, while he drives, he dictates thoughts, notes, and letters to a tape recorder, so even his drive time is utilized efficiently.

Jeanette attributes her extra time to making lists. At the end of each workday, she makes a list of things to do the next day. She organizes her tasks so there will be no duplication of efforts, no backtracking, and no wasted motions. She also makes lists for her personal activities, such as making a shopping list so she can buy everything she needs for the week in just one trip, rather than needing to make several trips.

Ken finds his extra time in small segments throughout the week. While others might waste fifteen minutes here, squander a half-hour there, or "kill" an hour, Ken uses these small segments of time to do something productive. In a week's time, Ken estimates these small segments add up to over fifteen hours.

Gail works a normal 8:00 to 5:00 schedule and spends the evening hours and weekends with her family and friends. But five nights a week she works from about 9:00 P.M. to midnight in the serenity of her home office.

The examples could go on, but you probably see a pattern. Many of those who work long hours set priorities for the use of their time, and work is a high priority. Nearly all make sacrifices to find the extra time, but the sacrifices of giving up television viewing, lunch in a restaurant, or chit-chatting with colleagues during the work day aren't major detriments. And they are organized. They don't fritter away their time.

Certainly, not everyone should aspire to work fifty, sixty, seventy or eighty hour weeks. For many, the forty hour workweek fits their goals, needs, and philosophy of life just fine. But, if you aspire to rise above the masses, to accomplish all that you can, and to do more than others, follow this simple rule — put in your time.

AS THE BOY SCOUTS SAY...

Here's the scenario: Adams Company has an opening for an assistant manager for its new store. It's a wonderful position with a high salary, terrific fringe benefits, generous paid vacations, profit sharing, bonuses, and an outstanding retirement program. And, historically at Adams, an assistant manager stays an assistant for only about two years and then becomes a manager. And then the pay and benefits really get good. After that, there's potential to become a district manager and, maybe eventually, an executive in the home office. It's a once-in-a-lifetime opportunity.

More than a hundred qualified people applied for the job. Adams has screened the applicants by studying their resumes and application letters and by checking references. The pool of applicants has been narrowed down to two people who will be interviewed. And, we get to watch.

The two finalists for the job are Mary and Cynthia. The education, experience, age, appearance, and overall background of the two applicants are remarkably similar. Therefore, it appears that the one who is the most impressive in the personal interview will get the job.

A team of three Adams' personnel will conduct the interview, an executive, a store manager, and someone from the Human Resources Department.

Mary is the first to be interviewed. Her grooming, dress, and bearing are perfect.

The interview begins with the interviewers describing the company philosophy and explaining the duties of the assistant manager. Then, the questions start.

"Why do you want this job?" asks the executive.

"I, ah, think it would be fun!" Mary answers.

"Tell me about yourself," says the Human Resources person.

"I have a mother and father and two brothers — and I like to play golf and tennis," Mary answers.

"What can you do for us?" asks the store manager.

"Well, I'll always be on time, and I'll work very hard, and I'll do the best I can," Mary replies.

"Why should we hire you?" asks the executive.

"Because, well, I'll work hard, and I'll try to be a good employee," Mary answers.

"What are your goals for ten years from now?" asks the store manager.

"Whew!" Mary says, "Ten years is a long time — I haven't made any real plans, but I guess I'd like to be married and have a couple of children."

The question and answer session is over and the three interviewers thank Mary for her time. They inform Mary that they will contact her on Wednesday of next week to let her know their decision.

Now, it's Cynthia's turn to be interviewed. Her grooming, dress, and bearing are perfect, just as Mary's was. The interviewers provide Cynthia with background information about the company and the job. And then they get down to the questions. The exact same questions asked of Mary.

"Why do you want this job?"

"I know Adams Company is one of the leaders in the retail field and is the second fastest growing company in the industry," Cynthia begins. "I believe it would be exciting and challenging to be a part of the Adams organization."

"Tell me about yourself."

Cynthia reaches into her attaché case and withdraws four copies of her resume. She gives one to each interviewer and keeps a copy for herself. Cynthia uses the resumé as a guide as she talks about her education, experience, personal interests, hobbies, and achievements.

"What can you do for us?"

"In my present position as manager of the clothing department at Baker Department Store, I have increased sales by forty five percent over the past two years. I did this by analyzing the products that sell and that don't sell and by ordering accordingly. I also instituted a "Clothing Club" that has led to more than 500 steady customers. I designed a quarterly newsletter to keep in touch with the Clothing Club members, to inform them of new fashion trends, to provide other information, and, of course, to tell them about our new merchandise. I believe I can bring some of these types of ideas to Adams, while still working within the marketing concept that has made Adams so successful."

"Why should we hire you?"

"I believe I have the educational background and experience to do the job," Cynthia says. "You will also find me to be dependable, hard-working, honest, loyal, and cooperative. I will put forth my very best effort and believe I can be a real asset to Adams Company."

"What are your goals for ten years from now?"

"My immediate goal, which I hope to accomplish within the next few months, is to secure an assistant manager's position in a retail department store like Adams," Cynthia begins. "Then, I would like to get enough experience in that position until I feel really comfortable and confident that I'm ready for the next step as a store manager. This may take two to five years. After that, I hope to become a store manager and be in that position ten years from now."

Cynthia's interview ends and the interviewers thank her for her time. They inform her that they will contact her on Wednesday of next week with their decision.

As stated earlier, Mary and Cynthia are very comparable in education, experience, age, appearance, and most other factors, so the decision of whom to hire will be based on the interview. You were there for the interviews. If it were your decision, which one would you hire?

It is obvious that Cynthia had the most impressive interview. Mary stammered a bit and gave short answers that revealed very little about her true abilities and potential. On the other hand, Cynthia gave very impressive, professional-sounding answers that were complete and provided insight into her accomplishments and capabilities.

Why do you suppose Cynthia interviewed so well and Mary did so poorly? The answer is simple — Cynthia *cheated*. She knew all of the interview questions in advance.

Well, she didn't really cheat in the normal sense of the word. You see, she made up her own list of potential questions before the interview. She anticipated questions that might be asked of her and developed answers in advance. Then, she had a friend help her rehearse for the interview by asking her those questions.

Cynthia's list of potential interview questions was thorough and many of the questions were tough and hard-hitting. Compared to the rehearsal sessions, the real interview with Adams Company was a snap. Here are Cynthia's questions:

"What are your interests?"

"Tell me about yourself."

"What do you like best about your present job?"

"What do you like least about your present job?"

"What can you do for us?"

"What do you feel makes you qualified for this job?"

"Why do you want this job?"

"Why did you apply for a job with our company?"

"Why should we hire you?"

"Do you have specific goals you want to accomplish here?"

"Are you willing to transfer?"

"How long do you intend to stay here?"

"What do you know about our company?"

"What do you do in your spare time?"

"What would you like to know about our company?"

"Why do you want to leave your present job?"

"What is your best quality?"

"What is your greatest weakness?"

"If you caught your best friend shoplifting merchandise from the store, what would you do?"

"As assistant manager, what would you do to promote team spirit among the employees in the store?"

"Would you mind working a few extra hours beyond your normal schedule once in a while?"

"Do you think most people are honest?"

"What upsets you the most?"

"Are you a leader or a follower?"

"Tell me how your education has prepared you for this job."

"What would you do if the store manager expected you to do all of your work and part of his, too?"

"How much money do you expect as starting pay?"

The story of Mary and Cynthia is interesting and revealing. They both spent thousands of hours studying to get an education, each spent thousands of hours working to gain experience, and each devoted countless hours developing a sense of grooming, dress, and bearing. Yet, when it really counted, Cynthia spent perhaps an additional forty or fifty hours preparing herself for the once-in-a-lifetime opportunity interview. Mary didn't. Cynthia got the job. Mary didn't.

Life is filled with events that really matter to us, at least at the moment. Maybe it's meeting one's prospective in-laws or the boss' wife for the first time. Maybe it's going to a parent-teacher conference, applying for a bank loan, or seeking an adjustment on defective merchandise. Perhaps it's applying for a job or asking for a pay raise. Whatever it is, when something important is on the horizon and it really matters to you, try to follow Cynthia's example, and the motto of the Boy Scouts — *Be Prepared*.

V.
MIGHTIER THAN THE SWORD

Some people can irritate others by simply saying, "Good Morning." Others open their mouths and golden words roll off their silver tongues.

Communication, or the lack of it, we should say, is the main reason for misunderstandings and arguments, for hurt feelings and hard feelings, for lawsuits and divorces.

Flat out, communicating clearly is difficult. However, there is hope. There are several simple techniques that you can use that will help you avoid some pitfalls and to improve your ability to say what you want.

> *Think like a wise man, but communicate in the language of the people.* William Yeats

> *Tell me and I'll forget. Show me, and I may not remember. Involve me, and I'll understand.* Native American proverb

> *A gossip is someone who talks to you about others, a bore is someone who talks to you about himself, and a brilliant conversationalist is someone who talks to you about yourself.* Lisa Kirk

> *There is only one rule for being a good talker — learn to listen.* Christopher Morley

> *Never explain — your friends do not need it and your enemies will not believe you anyway.* Elbert Hubbard

Tell the truth, and so puzzle and confound your adversaries. Henry Woton

Many a true word is spoken in jest. English proverb

You may easily play a joke on a man who likes to argue — agree with him. Ed Howe

It usually takes more than three weeks to prepare a good impromptu speech. Mark Twain

Never praise a sister to a sister in the hope of your compliments reaching the proper ears. Rudyard Kipling

Composers should write tunes that chauffeurs and errand boys can whistle. Thomas Beecham

One of the lessons of history is that nothing is often a good thing to do and always a clever thing to say. Will Durant

A WAY WITH WORDS

You may recall the incident. It was during baseball's World Series, and a pitcher was thrown out of the game for swearing. If you want the full story, you can check the newspapers. Try October, 1990. This is just a quick news capsule.

The pitcher threw a pitch that was called a "ball" by the umpire. The pitcher, of course, thought it was a "strike." So, the pitcher cut loose with a few choice swear words to let the umpire know that he was damned unhappy with the call. Without hesitation, the umpire ejected the pitcher from the game.

The ejecting of the pitcher for swearing caused quite a stir, and the team's manager stormed the field and argued vehemently with the umpire. More swearing took place, but no one was ejected for it this time.

This raises the question, what was so special about the pitcher's swearing that it got him ejected from the game? After all, professional baseball players aren't exactly Cub Scouts, and they've been known to swear a little from time to time.

A few days later, the behind-the-scenes story came out. The pitcher hadn't just sworn, he had sworn at the umpire. And, as it was explained, it's an unwritten rule that it's permissible for a player to swear, but not to swear at an umpire. That'll get you ejected.

As an old pro explained it, if the player is upset with the umpire's call and says to the umpire, "That was a strike, you dirty S.O.B.," that'll get them ejected.

Then, the old pro described the proper wording that the player should have used, which would have allowed him to let the umpire know what he thought of the call without getting thrown out of the game. That wording is, "If that wasn't a strike, *I'm* a dirty S.O.B." Now, that's finesse!

THE SILENT LINGO

I just figured it out five minutes ago. I've spent approximately 22,680 hours speaking in front of groups of people. This includes teaching in high school and college, presenting seminars, and spouting off on a variety of topics anytime I could muster an audience. And, I estimate my average audience to be 36.3 persons. So that amounts to 823,284 person-hours that people have sat there looking at me while I talk.

And, while they've been looking at me, I've been looking at them. I've seen some amazing things in those 823,284 person-hours, believe me, including a few things that would make a Marine blush. But mostly, I've observed the *little* differences in how people sit, how they hold their heads, how they occupy their hands, how they position their feet and legs, and what their eyes do. The little things people do when they don't say anything, but that say a lot. *The silent lingo.*

Oh, yes, the silent lingo, sometimes called *body language*. It can often send a message stronger and more directly than any words might. It can send a message that reflects the sender's honest and true feelings, because often the senders, themselves, don't even know that they're sending a message. This silent lingo can tell someone if you're interested or disinterested, if you're happy or unhappy, if you agree or disagree, if you approve or disapprove. The silent lingo can win you friends and job promotions, or, on the other hand, it can ruin relationships or get you fired. It's that powerful.

We all use this silent lingo, body language, to send messages constantly. But many people, I've learned from observation, are either not aware of this language or do not know how to use it to their advantage.

So, if you can identify this silent lingo, corral it and put it to work for you. You can send powerful positive messages to others that will reap great rewards for you. Here's how you can do it.

Suppose you work at a company, and your boss is conducting a meeting. There are thirty of you in attendance. Each of you wants to favorably impress the boss since that could eventually result in a pay raise, a promotion, or some other plumb.

All thirty of you are sitting in your chairs looking at the boss and the boss is in the front of the room looking at the thirty of you. And here's the sorry sight the boss sees.

"There's a few apple polishers who agree with every stupid thing I say and roar at every lame joke I tell. It makes me sick. There's the two guys sitting in the back making snide comments to each other, probably about me, thinking I don't notice because they've got their hands cupped over their mouths. There's the two gigglers slyly passing a piece of paper back and forth. They try to mask their laughter with a cough now and then as they read the latest one-liner and inhale the new caricature of me on the paper. There's the sloucher — by God, I hope he does-n't hurt himself and sue me when he finally falls out of that chair. There's the deadpan — her mind is in neutral, and her eyes must be propped open with toothpicks. And there's somebody who just snuck in the back door. And who's that guy with all the gold chains and bracelets and rings — have I got a pimp on the pay-roll?"

"And who's that fashion plate with the long fingernails? Nobody dressed like that could possibly get down in the trenches and dig into any work — might get messed up. And that guy's fill-ing his notebook with sketches of sunsets — I paid a dollar and half for that damn notebook. And I'll bet, if I pulled that guy's fist out from under his chin, his head would drop so fast he'd get a nosebleed. And that smell in the room has just got to be from her shoes — I wish she'd either put them back on or sit on her feet. And what's that guy doing over there — and that woman here in front? They actually seem interested. They're sitting up straight and watching me and listening to me. What's that they're writing in their notebooks? Why, they're taking notes — actually writing down those golden words of wisdom that roll off my silver tongue. They're awake and alert. They appear like they actually want to be here. Hey, I've got the attention of two people out of thirty. Not bad. I've still got the touch."

So, here's a group of thirty people, all sending a constant bar-rage of silent messages to the boss. Perhaps many of these people are far more interested than it appears, but that really doesn't mat-ter. What does matter is how this behavior *appears* to the boss and how the boss interprets the messages being sent to him.

Therefore, your goal should be to send silent messages to the boss, or to whomever you're dealing with, through body language that will appear positive and that will be interpreted favorably. It's easy to do. All is takes is a little conscious effort and a little practice.

Let's start with where people sit in the room. I've never really figured out if its true that the most interested people sit in the front and the least interested sit in the back. But, it really doesn't matter if it's true, either. That's because most speakers seem to believe its true — so it does make it true as far as they're concerned. So, sit in the front. You'll appear interested.

Next, look at your clothes. Do you look like a pimp, hooker, mortician, beachcomber, clotheshorse, or tourist? That's fine if that's what you're supposed to look like; but if it's not, it's not. Dress the part.

How about the way you sit in your chair. Are you sitting up straight with both feet on the floor or with legs appropriately crossed? Slouchers look lazy and disinterested. Leaners look like they're exhausted or hung over.

Where are your arms? If they're folded in front of you, it appears you're blocking out the speaker and their message. If they're clasped behind your head, you look like you think you're in charge or think you're better than the others in the room, including the speaker. If they're dangling at your sides, you look like you're on vacation, not ready to pitch in and work. Rest your hands in your lap or on the table in front of you. Better yet, put them to productive use taking notes.

Hold your head erect. If you let your head droop, you look tired or bored. If you must prop your head up with your hand, don't do it by placing your fist against your cheek — you look sad or mad and appear bored to death. Rather, place your index finger along the outside of your cheek, place your thumb under your chin, and curl the remaining three fingers. You'll look interested, intelligent, and alert. Practice in the mirror; you'll see what I mean.

And the most important part, the eyes. Don't let them wander around the room or become fixed in a stare. Rather, look at the speaker with some life and fire in your eyes — but don't burn a hole through the other person. It is said that the eyes are the windows to the soul, so let the other person see that your soul, and your heart, is into this thing, whatever it is.

And, when you walk, walk like you're going somewhere. And always carry something in your hand — it will look like you're going somewhere on a mission. And, make your handshake firm and brief, accompanied with eye contact. Well, these are but a few insights into the silent lingo, but you probably get the message.

Just remember, even if you're not interested in what's going on, even if you hate being where you are and doing what you're doing, you can use the silent lingo to finesse 'em into thinking that you really do care, because it *appears* that you do. And what appears to be true to the other person will, in fact, be true to them, even if it's not true.

TRUTH VARIES

Sharon was driving down a residential street with her two young children in the back seat. The children were becoming increasingly unruly and had ignored her pleas for them to behave. So, Sharon turned her head for just a moment to give them a dourful stare and to yell at them. She even took a swat at the children, but missed.

Just then, a car backed out of a driveway and hit Sharon's car in the side. It wasn't much of a collision and no one was injured. But it doesn't take much of a collision to cause $2,000 damage.

Neither driver's insurance company wanted to accept responsibility for fixing Sharon's car so the case ended up in court, about a year after the accident.

Sharon's state follows what is called the *comparative negligence theory*. That is, if both drivers are partly at fault, the court decides what percent of fault each has and divides up the cost accordingly. But, if one driver is totally at fault and the other driver has no fault, the guilty party must pay the full cost.

There were no witnesses to the accident, so Sharon and the other driver were the only ones to testify at the trial.

As we know, Sharon was looking in the back seat trying to discipline her children and didn't see the other car backing out of the driveway. If she had been watching the road, she would have seen the car and probably could have avoided the accident. So, we know Sharon is partly at fault and under the comparative negligence theory, should pay part of the damage costs — maybe half.

Sharon took the witness stand and described the accident. When asked if she was watching the road or if her attention had been momentarily diverted, she calmly stated that, yes, she was watching the road. Yes, she had both hands on the wheel. And, no, nothing had diverted her attention.

The other driver could not dispute Sharon's claim, because, after all, he had not even seen Sharon's car coming.

The verdict was announced — Sharon won. The other driver was totally at fault and must pay the entire cost of fixing Sharon's car.

But we know the truth — Sharon lied. Or, did she?

Sharon's version of the accident wasn't the way it really happened, but Sharon didn't lie.

In the year between when the accident occurred and when the matter came to trial, Sharon simply came to recall the accident a little differently. Oh, sure, she remembered turning around to look into the back seat and recalled yelling at the kids. But, the more she thought about it, that was several moments before the accident. By the time the accident occurred, she had already returned her attention to the road and was in full control of the car. And then she was hit. Yes. That's the way it was. And that's the way Sharon honestly believes it happened.

My writer friend, Steve Kammerer, was a guest lecturer addressing a college journalism class. His topic was "Truth in Journalism." Steve was about forty-five minutes into his presentation when the door swung open, someone rushed in, said a few words, pulled out a gun, and shot Steve. Steve dropped to the floor like a sack of potatoes, and the assailant quickly disappeared out the door.

Half the class was screaming, and the other half sat in stunned silence, bordering on shock.

But they all screamed, and then applauded, when Steve picked himself up off the floor and took a bow.

"Now," he said, "I want you to take out a sheet of paper and write a news story on what you just witnessed."

When the students were finished with their stories, they discussed them. Even though they had all witnessed the same event, the reports varied widely. Most identified the assailant as a man, but two thought it was a woman. The height ranged from 5' 9" to 6' 2" and the weight varied from 140 to 200 pounds. The assailant's clothing was remembered as being black, green, blue, tan, brown, and orange. All but one reported that Steve had been shot. That reporter recalled seeing Steve get knifed and identified the loud bang as coming from Steve's head hitting the desk when he fell.

The words said by the assailant were repeated as "I finally found you," "I fondly fined you," "A pound of fondue," "A potato's hound tooth," "I'm gonna shoot you," "You cheatin' snafoo," and "Hello to you, too."

And, very few of the would-be reporters recalled how and when the assailant exited the room.

Here's another example, I had just finished presenting a day-long's writer's seminar. Everyone had left the auditorium except for a grandmotherly-looking woman of about sixty-five who had been slowly packing, unpacking, and repacking her papers — apparently she wanted to talk to me.

"Mr. Davidson," she said "I know you said you don't have time at a seminar like this to read and critique anyone's writing, but I have something here I'd like you to look at. Since everyone's gone now, they'll never know."

She described that the sheet of paper she was handing me was the introduction to a book she was writing. She had originally written it as a two-page introduction she had shown it to a friend who told her it rambled on a bit and might be better as a snappier one-page introduction. She rewrote it as one page and showed it to someone else who thought it was kind of short and recommended that she rewrite it as two pages. She rewrote it as two pages and showed it to someone else who thought it was a little wordy and suggested that she rewrite it as a lively one-page intro. And now I had that one-page version in my hand.

"Mr. Davidson," she said, "will you tell me what to do."

I gave her best advice I was capable of giving. I told her that she would have to decide. That she would have to determine what she was trying to accomplish in writing that introduction and then be able to recognize when she had met her goal. And when she had done that, the introduction would be complete and appropriate, regardless of what the length happened to be.

Everyone wants to know the truth. In some cases, there is a definite, absolute, undeniable truth. In other situations, though, truth varies. It varies with our perception, our expectations, and our circumstances. So, if we are waiting for someone to tell us "the truth," we may never hear it. For truth, like beauty, is often in the eye of the beholder.

YOU'RE ON TRIAL—ADMIT NOTHING

Harvey was subpoenaed to testify as a witness at a trial, so he went to his attorney for advice. For $150, his attorney gave him this counsel: "Admit nothing."

Harvey received good advice, well worth the money. And it is advice that all of us would do well to follow in our daily lives, for we are constantly on trial and are continually being judged. Often we admit things, to our detriment, when others haven't even asked for a confession.

I recall, for instance, being at a meeting where the chairperson asked a man for his opinion on a particular matter. The answer didn't require facts, figures, or special knowledge, just a personal opinion.

"I'm dumb," the man said sincerely, "but if it were me I'd... "

The man's comments actually made a lot of sense, but nobody listened. He had already confessed to being dumb and who in their right mind would pay any attention to, or agree with, the comments of a dumb person. And he wasn't surprised nobody listened, either, because, after all, he was dumb. As a result, he felt even dumber.

A short time ago, I attended a seminar where there were about fifty people in attendance. The speaker walked to the podium and began by saying, "Good morning. I don't feel very well today, but I'll do the best I can."

The speaker didn't realize it, but she had just announced that she was not going to give a very good presentation that day and that we weren't going to get our money's worth.

The senior class of a small high school was nominating candidates for homecoming queen.

"I nominate Joanie," a young man said.

It was a good choice. Joanie, although not beautiful, was nice-looking and was one of the most popular girls in school. She would make a very good homecoming queen.

Joanie shook her head and said, "I'm not pretty enough to be homecoming queen."

The class responded predictably — Joanie wasn't elected as one of the queen candidates.

At the same school a week later, the homecoming pep rally was held on Thursday night. After the pep rally, "Spike" and two of his friends drove past the principal's house and tossed a couple of pumpkins onto the lawn, which exploded all over the place.

It was a schoolboy prank, and it didn't cause any real harm. It didn't even upset the principal. He knew the students would pull some prank, they did every year, and this was one of the milder ones.

The next morning, the principal called Spike into his office. Spike fretted and worried about what punishment might await him, and he decided to plead for leniency.

Spike walked into the principal's office and said, "I'm sorry I threw those pumpkins onto your lawn last night — we didn't mean anything by it."

The principal's face broke out in a huge grin. "Spike," he said, "I called you to my office to ask if you'd drive the convertible for the homecoming queen in the parade today, but I appreciate your telling me about the pumpkins — I wondered who did that."

Spike missed the homecoming parade — he was sanding desks in the library.

At the company where Jill works management tries to create a friendly atmosphere.

"How are you this morning!" Jill's boss said cheerfully.

"I'm really tired," Jill replied. "Billy has the croup, and I was up with him half the night."

The boss's comment wasn't actually intended as a question to be answered literally, as Jill did. It was meant to be a cheerful, enthusiastic greeting, with the expectation that Jill would reply in kind. Since Jill had admitted to being tired and dragging, though, the boss silently vowed to keep an eye on Jill and to prod her a bit to make sure she stayed awake and did her job.

Glenn and Travis worked for the same company and were friendly rivals for the sales manager's position that would become vacant soon, or so they thought.

One cold, winter morning Glenn entered the office bundled up from head to toe. He began complaining about the bitter cold and how it chilled him straight to the bone.

Travis smiled inwardly. Glenn had just admitted to a weakness — he couldn't accept certain unavoidable and unchangeable situations. Travis knew that he would be the next sales manager, not Glenn.

Linda Klein is a professor at the State University. She gave a ten question essay midterm exam to her sociology class. With fifty students in the class, that's 500 questions to read, evaluate, and grade. Professor Klein is conscientious, but, still, she tries to grade the papers as quickly as she can so she can return the test papers to the students at the next class session. Therefore, instead of carefully reading and studying every golden word of wisdom written by each student, she often scans the answers looking for key words, concepts, and phrases.

Take Doug's answer to the question, "What are reference groups?" When Professor Klein read the answer, there were several key words and phrases, and it looked like a pretty good answer. She was about to give him seven points. That is, until she got to the end of the answer where Doug had written a personal note to Professor Klein, "Well, am I close?"

Doug's note, although intended to be light-hearted, revealed that he didn't know the answer, was guessing, and apparently didn't expect to earn any points. Professor Klein re-read Doug's answer, carefully, and found that, although Doug had used some of the right terms, he was horribly confused about what they meant and how they related to the concept of reference groups. Doug got zero points.

In each of the foregoing scenarios, a person blundered by revealing information that wasn't asked for, much to their own detriment. If they had simply kept their mouths shut or, in some cases, waited until they were required to reveal the information, they would have been much better off. There is an old proverb that illustrates the point: "Tis better to keep quiet and to be thought ignorant than to open your mouth and remove all doubt."

THE SELF-ORDAINED

Gary Clobature is the town's real estate expert. Ask anybody, and they'll tell you it's true — Gary is the expert.

It's interesting how Gary got to be the expert, particularly when at least half of the real estate brokers in town know as much about real estate as Gary. Maybe more.

It all started when Gary was chitchatting with a reporter from the local newspaper. The reporter casually asked how the real estate market was doing, and Gary explained that, while the nationwide market was in a slump, the local market was booming. Then Gary suggested that local residents might be interested in a news article on this topic and offered to provide background information and research data if the reporter wanted to write such a story. The reporter agreed it was a good idea, and she wrote the story, quoting Gary profusely throughout.

Gary sent a copy of the article to the news director at one of the local radio stations. He liked the story and carried an abbreviated version, again, quoting Gary.

After that, whenever the newspaper reporter, the radio station news director, or anyone else wanted information on real estate, they called Gary. Or, if Gary thought there was something particularly newsworthy, he called them.

Somewhere along the line, Gary adopted the slogan for his real estate company, "The Real Estate Experts." He uses the slogan in all of his advertising and has it printed on his office stationery, business cards, and other business papers.

So, how did Gary Clobature get to be the real estate expert? He was appointed. And, who appointed him? Gary Clobature did, that's who.

Ann Mills is the best mother in town. Some say she's the best mother in the world. But there wasn't a contest, or anything like that, to determine who was the best mother. That title was simply given to Ann. And who gave it to her? Her husband did, by telling all of his friends, and relatives, and anyone else who would listen what a wonderful mother Ann was. And then they told their friends and relatives, and it sort of mushroomed from there. Oh, Ann's a good mother all right, but, then, she has to be. She's got quite a reputation to live up to.

Then, there is George. He's intelligent. You can tell by his round wire-rimmed glasses, his professional clothing, and his tousled hairdo. If that isn't proof enough, look at those books he's carrying — Aristotle and heavy thinkers like that. Oh, when you talk to him, George doesn't come off as being any smarter than anyone else, but he's probably holding it all back because one thing's for sure, he's an intellect. You can tell it just by looking at him.

And then there's Huckelberry. Huckleberry is the best bartender in town. Well, to be honest, he may not be the best, but he's the flashiest, which some people seem to equate with being the best. And since there's really no way of measuring who's the best, let's simply assume Huckleberry is. Because he is the flashiest, and that we can measure.

In truth, none of the four people described in the preceding stories were more competent, skillful, or knowledgeable than any of their contemporaries. But everyone thinks they are because, somehow or other, they were ordained to their roles, either by themselves or by someone else close to them.

Few people in life seem to receive the recognition and admiration they deserve for their efforts and accomplishments. If you simply sit back and wait for others to recognize your achievements and to hand you accolades, it may be a long wait, like forever. But, if you want to be known as the leader, or the best, or the greatest you can be. First, learn what you're doing so you deserve your exalted title. Then, ordain yourself. And let me be among the first to congratulate you!

TAKE ME, TAKE ME

I recently saw the results of a poll that asked several hundred adults this question: "What single thing in life do you fear most?" Think about it for a moment — how would you answer this question?

One might assume that the top response to the questions might be "Death," or "Losing my job," or "Becoming terminally ill," or "Being tragically injured," or "Spending eternity in Hell," or something like that. Oh, they were on the list all right, but the top item, the number one fear, was — get this — "Getting up and speaking in front of a group."

I understand this. As a youth in junior high and in high school, just being told by the teacher that each of us would have to make a speech in class made me go pale. I couldn't sleep for several nights before my scheduled speech. When I finally was called upon to get up in front of the group, my complexion was a clammy gray, my whole body broke out in a cold sweat, and my legs were like rubber. Couple all of this with a cottonmouth and a thick tongue, and you can see why I dreaded making speeches in front of the class and why I was horrible at it.

By the time I graduated from college, I was a little more used to giving speeches in front of a group, but I still didn't like it and still wasn't good at it. In fact, we had to take one speech class as a requirement for graduation, and I put it off until my final semester — and then I took it as a night class, thinking, somehow, that would make it easier. It didn't.

That was all years ago, and I have finally become comfortable speaking in front of a group. I even do it *voluntarily* these days, being one of America's most active writer's seminar presenters. And, I enjoy it. I love it.

But, I still remember the fear that gripped me when I was required to get up and speak in front of a group. I've done a lot of thinking about it and have come to a few conclusions about why this fear exists in so many people and just what can be done to overcome it or, at least, to lessen it.

I developed most of this theory about how to overcome the fear of giving a speech when I was a college teacher. As soon as I assigned a speech or report as an assignment, I could see about half the class go pale right on the spot. When it came time for the in-class presentation and I asked for volunteers, everybody looked down, fearing that any eye contact with me might be misconstrued as a willingness to be called upon. And when I did call someone's name, that person would either freeze or go limp, and everyone else would heave a sigh of relief, at least temporarily.

The speakers were almost all the same — clammy gray, sweating, pale, cottonmouthed, thick-tongued, and rubber legged. But, after their speech was over, every speaker reacted about the same — relieved, exhilarated, smiling, laughing, free. They felt great. It was over. They had survived this horrible, life-threatening obstacle. And it really wasn't so bad, after all — now that it was done.

So, here's my solution for how to overcome the fear of giving a speech in front of a group. Actually, a small part of my solution deals with overcoming the fear — that will probably always be there. The main part of the solution deals with making it *appear* that you have no fear of getting up and speaking in front of the group. The idea is, it doesn't really matter how you know you feel. What's important is how others perceive you as feeling about making this speech. (That's why I call my solution a *theory* — okay?)

First, when you know you've got to make a speech in front of a group, accept it. Don't fret about it, don't devise schemes to avoid it when you know you can't, and don't tell everybody you see that you're worried about making this speech. Remember, they're terrified of making speeches in front of a group, and they'll only add to your hysteria.

Second, get well prepared in advance. Do your research. Develop some notes or make an outline to use as a guide. Then rehearse and keep rehearsing until you're confident that you've got good material and that you know how to deliver it. And when you give your speech, use your notes.

Third, and this is the big one, when it's time for the presentations to begin, realize this — you are going to have to make your speech, sooner or later. So don't sit there fretting and stewing, waiting to be called on. *Volunteer — immediately*. It will lessen the tension considerably, and, most importantly, it will make it *appear* to everyone in the room that you're not afraid at all of making this speech. All the other erstwhile speakers will admire you and wish they had your courage and freedom of fear from this dreaded punishment. Your teacher or boss, or whoever got you into this, will appreciate your jumping in to get the ball rolling and will reward you accordingly.

Fourth, walk up to the podium like you own it. Strong, confident steps. Take a few deep breaths to relax. Even if you hate being there and even if you're scared out of your wits, don't admit anything. Just go ahead with your presentation like you've practiced. Oh, sure, you may be shaking inside, and you may be sweating and cottonmouthed, but no one will know but you.

When it's over, you can calmly go sit back down and relax. You can watch the rest of them as they squirm and suffer, sitting there waiting to be called upon to be executed.

AND, THERE WAS SILENCE

There are several ways to approach a discussion, debate, or argument — whatever you want to call it. You can use logic and try to win your case by appealing to your adversary's sense of reason. Or you can prove your argument is true by using hard facts, statistics, and figures.

Perhaps you can overrun them with a verbal barrage until they cave in. Or you might refute everything they say and prove them wrong — and, thus, you right. Or you might overpower them with intimidation. Perhaps you could outlast them, simply staying awake longer. Or maybe you can steamroll them with a combination of facts, theories, intimidation, wit, charm, and endurance.

But then, again, you might win your discussion by using one of the most effective, but least-used, techniques, silence. Yes, silence. When used properly, it can be more effective than any of the yelling, screaming, desk pounding, intimidating, running-off-at-the-mouth techniques. It is the epitome of using the finesse 'em approach instead of the sledgehammer approach. Here's how it works.

Cathy was a real estate sales agent in California. She had been working with her client, Bill, for over six months, trying to find just the right building for his furniture emporium.

Finally, the perfect building became available, and Cathy called Bill immediately. Cathy and Bill viewed the building, and Cathy provided Bill with all the necessary information — zoning data, real estate tax and insurance amounts, utility costs, and everything else he needed. Bill asked if he could have an architect inspect the building, and Cathy encouraged him to do so.

Two days later, Cathy and Bill met to discuss the possible purchase of the building by Bill. It was everything Bill had described that he wanted, and more. The location, building size and design, parking facilities, and highway access were perfect. The real estate taxes, utilities, insurance, and other costs were reasonable. And the best part was that the price was a bargain and the terms were outstanding.

Cathy viewed all of the information with Bill. Yes, he agreed, everything met his requirements. Cathy tried a trial close, but Bill failed to make an offer to buy. Cathy again reviewed all the information with Bill and tried another trial close. Still no forthcoming offers. Sensing that she may have missed some key selling point, Cathy reviewed everything for a third time and tried another trial close, but no offer. They talked and discussed the project and talked some more, but still no offer from Bill.

Cathy knew that, if Bill didn't act that day, someone else would most likely buy the property, and Bill would regret it the rest of his life. And Cathy would lose her commission. So she decided to try a different approach.

"Bill," she said, "this building is perfect for your needs. The location, size, design, parking, and highway access are ideal. The taxes, insurance, and utilities are reasonable. The price is a bargain, the terms are outstanding, and you can afford it. It's just what you've been looking for. It will be good for you. Why don't we go ahead."

And then Cathy shut her mouth and didn't say another word.

They sat there in silence. Bill fidgeted and turned red and began to sweat. Cathy said nothing. She simply sat there calmly looking at Bill. She had asked him a question, and it was his turn to speak. Bill fidgeted some more and turned a brighter red and sweated some more. For twenty-five minutes they sat in silence like this.

Finally, Bill said, "I think you're right. Let's go ahead."

Bill had made a wonderful purchase, and Cathy had made a terrific sale.

Later, Cathy said, "I had said everything I knew, several times, and was getting nowhere. I knew it was ideal for Bill's needs, and he knew it, too. But it was a big decision, and he was hesitant. He needed time to think, and he couldn't do that while I was talking. So I simply shut my mouth. I was determined not to break the silence. I would have sat there for hours, days if necessary."

When I was teaching in college, I used silence as a technique from time to time to get a student to respond to a question I had asked.

I began to notice that I was slipping into a pattern that was not beneficial to my students. I would call a student's name and ask them a question. If the student put their head down and didn't answer in a few moments and it looked like no answer was forthcoming, I would simply call on someone else. Or I'd answer my own question. This got the student off the hook, perhaps saved them a little embarrassment, and moved the class along. But I came to realize it was not in the best interests of that student. The student was there to learn, to participate, and to express their ideas, and I was robbing them of those opportunities. Oh, I'm sure they appreciated my calling on someone else, but it was not good for their academic growth.

So I developed a new philosophy. If I asked a question that called for a factual answer, based on the textbook or lecture notes, and the student didn't answer, I passed over them in favor of someone else. If they didn't know the facts, they didn't, and no amount of waiting them out would change that. But if the question called for a personal opinion, which anyone could have, I waited them out in silence until they answered. Oh, sometimes it took a while, but I always got an answer. And, my students were better off because of it.

Next time you're in a discussion or debate or argument, consider using silence as a highly effective technique, or weapon, if you will. First, build a strong case for your position based on solid research, facts, and irrefutable evidence. Next, review the information with your adversary or make some type of summary statement. Then, ask them one final question. And then shut your mouth.

And, remember, he or she who breaks the silence, loses.

VI.
AVOIDING BOOBY TRAPS, PITFALLS, AND ALL MANNERS OF MUCK

Sometimes, life seems like you're walking across a battlefield loaded with land mines. One mis-step and you're scuttled.

Just think how much more pleasant and fun your life would be if you could sidestep just one, or maybe even two, of those booby traps per month.

Of course, we're not talking about real land mines or life-endangering booby traps. We're talking about something more serious than that — avoiding awkward or unpleasant situations in your day-to-day life. Or, at least they seem more serious at the moment.

Well, you can often avoid those awkward and unpleasant situations and have fun doing it at the same time. Sometimes, a lot of fun.

So live that you wouldn't be ashamed to sell the family parrot to the town gossip. Will Rogers

Confess your sins to the Lord and you will be forgiven; confess them to men, and you will be laughed at. Josh Billings

If you don't have time to do it right, you must have time to do it over. Anonymous

He who trusts secrets to a servant makes him his master. John Dryden

Fool me once, shame on you; fool me twice, shame on me. Anonymous

100

Don't tell me that worry doesn't do any good. I know better. The things I worry about don't happen. Anonymous

If you tell the truth, you don't have to remember anything. Mark Twain

One drink is just right, two is too many, three is not enough. Spanish proverb

One should never trust a woman who tells her age. A woman who would tell that would tell one anything. Oscar Wilde

Those who have free seats at a play hiss first. Chinese proverb

When a man's dog turns against him, it is time for a wife to pack her trunk and go home to Mama. Mark Twain

If you have screwed up and must now eat shit, don't nibble. Peter Knott

I don't know the key to success, but the key to failure is trying to please everybody. Bill Cosby

Eating words has never given me indigestion. Winston Churchill

THE SCANDAL THAT WASN'T

Country music entertainer Porter Wagoner was an established star with his own television program when he discovered a cute, perky blonde with huge bosoms. She could also sing — Dolly Parton was her name.

Dolly became a regular on The Porter Wagoner Show and became immensely popular. Eventually, Dolly left the show and skyrocketed to fame as one of the entertainment industry's brightest stars of music and movies. Most likely, you know who Dolly Parton is and have admired her talents.

Several years after Dolly left The Porter Wagoner Show and went off on her own, Wagoner wrote his autobiography. In it, he claimed that he had had an ongoing affair with Dolly while she was on his television show. He even identified their favorite motel and gave other details.

Wagoner's autobiography was published at the time when Dolly was at the peak of her career. Since Dolly had always enjoyed a wholesome image, free from any hint of improprieties or scandal, Wagoner's revelations held the potential of a bombshell that could blow her career apart, or, at least, tarnish her golden image.

Dolly was approached by a reporter and asked point blank if Porter Wagoner's accusations of an affair were true. Dolly was faced with a dilemma. If she admitted it to end any further speculation, well, that might hurt her career and could possibly open the door to all sorts of rumors connecting her with every man she'd ever met. If she denied it, it might only inspire reporters to try to prove it was true, and who knows what sensational headlines might appear next, even if there was nothing to the accusations.

Dolly handled the reporter's question with great tact and finesse. She simply smiled and said, "I'm not going to answer that, and I'm just going to let people think what they want. Half of them won't believe it, and the other half will just think I had bad taste."

Bravo, Dolly! End of scandal.

PROMISE YOU WON'T REPEAT THIS...

How many times have you told someone a deep, dark secret or some good, juicy gossip and sworn them to secrecy? Have they honored your request, or did they blab it all over town? Odds are that they passed the story along within five minutes — and added a new twist or embellishment of their own, to boot.

Sometimes, stating your opinion to a friend or co-worker can come back to haunt you. This is particularly true if they pass your comments along down the line, and it gets back to your boss or whoever is the subject of your comments.

Of course, we could keep our mouth shut and never say anything — that way we wouldn't have to fear defending ourselves when confronted with our own words. But who can do that? And, besides, often discussing and debating with others helps us to grow and learn and to focus our own thinking.

But, the question remains — how do you keep the other person from spreading your statements all over the place like cheap fertilizer?

Well, a friend of mine, Bob, is a master of getting people to keep their mouths shut and to not quote his comments to others. And, he does it with one simple little phrase.

I remember the time, many years ago, when Bob and I first got acquainted. We worked together, and there was an impending merger on the horizon. Rumors and theories were running rampant.

Bob had a particularly insightful vision of how this merger was going to take place and how it would affect virtually every individual in our department. But communicating this information to others in the department or in the company could cause Bob a lot of trouble or even get him fired.

Bob shared this information with me anyway, since he thought I needed to know it to make an informed decision of whether to accept another job offered to me or to stay put.

When Bob finished telling me what he knew, he looked me in the eye and said, "If you quote me, I'll deny it."

"If you quote me, I'll deny it." If I shoot off my mouth and tell others what Bob said and they ask him about it or confront him, he'll deny ever having said it. And they'll, most likely, believe him. Then they'll turn their anger and wrath to me. And I'll be the guy spreading rumors and having to defend himself.

"Well, I'll show him," I said to myself. "I won't tell a soul. That way I won't get myself in trouble."

And I never did tell anyone. Furthermore, I know a lot of people who know Bob, but I've never heard anyone quote him on anything that could cause Bob even the slightest uneasiness or embarrassment.

So, there's Bob's little secret — and it works. But, I'm not sure Bob would want me telling you this, so if you quote me, I'll deny it.

TENNIS, ANYONE?

It was a real coup. No one in the history of the sports world had ever pulled off such a matchup. The number one and number two rated tennis players in the world would play each other on national television in a winner-take-all match for $100,000. The loser gets nothing.

The sponsoring television network, who put the dream match together, lost no time promoting it as the greatest tennis match of all time. A real duel. A real battle. With the winner-take-all stakes, you knew both players would give it all they had.

The network had truly scooped its competition and was making the most of it with an extensive advertising campaign. Public interest was building. A winner-take-all tennis match was like a fight to the death, and you know how much fun that is.

Things were going along smoothly until a competing network broke its story about a week before the big match. Reliable sources had informed them that it wasn't a winner-take-all match after all — each player was to receive the same amount regardless of who won. And they had a copy of the contract between the network and the tennis players to prove it.

If the story was untrue, the network sponsoring the tennis match would have received a free once-in-a-lifetime publicity windfall that one can only dream about and ratings would no doubt double, or triple — everybody would tune in to watch the match. And, this, all delivered by a nosey competitor.

On the other hand, if the story was true, the sponsoring network was in a real bind.

It would have been fun to sit in on the strategy session of the network bigwigs discussing how to handle this crisis. Since we weren't there, we can only surmise that the options they came up with were similar to the following:

1. Deny. Deny. Deny. However, if the other network does have a copy of the contract showing it wasn't a winner-take-all match as advertised, we'll really look bad, and it may take years to recover.

2. Do nothing. Wait for it to blow over. But, in the meantime, all of our competitors will have a real heyday crucifying us until the match is over, and even beyond.

3. Point the finger at somebody down the chain of command somewhere; heap all of the blame on them, and make a big deal out of firing them. Maybe we could even have a public flogging. But the guy who got fired might point his finger back up the chain of command, and it could get messy.

4. Have someone in a position of real authority, like the network president, go on television and take full responsibility for misleading the public.

Well, if you were in on the strategy session, which of the four options would you recommend?

As it turned out, the story was true — it wasn't a winner-take-all match after all.

The network chose option number four. The network president went on television during prime time and solemnly and totally admitted the facts — it wasn't a winner-take-all match. The network had deceived the public. They had no excuses, they were sorry, and they would work hard to regain the public trust and to see nothing like this ever happened again.

End of story. Once the network totally, fully, completely admitted their wrongdoing, none of the competing networks any longer had a story, it was all over. Once the public knew the full story, there was nothing new to tell them.

So as the quote by Peter Knott at the beginning of this section says, "If you screwed up and must now eat it, don't nibble." Or something like that.

By the way, do you recall which network promoted that ill-fated, winner-take-all tennis match? I don't. The strategy worked.

FEEL FREE TO CALL ANYTIME

Three professional women drove to a meeting in a city about 100 miles from home. They left about a half-hour early since Angie wanted to drop off her computer at a service center in that city.

The women parked the car about a half block from the computer service center. The other two women offered to help, but Angie said she could manage to carry the computer by herself.

Angie was struggling to wiggle the boxed computer from the back seat of the car when a man — a gentleman — came along and offered his assistance. Angie graciously accepted.

Now, Angie is a beautiful woman. Tall, slender, gorgeous hair, sharp facial features, sparkling eyes, dazzling smile. It was obvious that the gentleman enjoyed coming to her rescue.

About ten minutes later, Angie and the gentleman emerged from the service center and returned to the car.

As she opened the car door, Angie said, "Thank you, so much for your assistance."

"Can I have your phone number?" the gentleman asked.

Angie opened her purse and pulled out a business card. She handed it to him and said, "Here's my husband's card. He's a lawyer. Feel free to call anytime."

THE SECRET

Joe had a secret that he vowed not to tell anyone — at least, not for now. Besides that, Joe was a little short of money. So, he made a list of people whom he considered to be close friends that he thought might possibly give him a small loan.

Joe approached each person on his list and asked for a loan of $100, which he promised to repay whenever he was able. The responses included the following:

> "No problem; pay it back whenever you can."

> "Whew, money's a little tight right now; I just couldn't come up with a hundred."

> "Here's the $100, don't worry about paying it back."

> "Are you sure a hundred's enough? I could spare a little more if you need."

> "Uh, well, uh, well, uh — do you think it's going to rain?"

So what did Joe do with the money he borrowed? Well, he threw a party — one heck of party. A party where he revealed his secret to all of his friends in attendance.

You see earlier in the week, Joe had won the lottery, with a cash prize of over $20 million. He suspected that, when the news got out, he'd have lots of people coming to him for loans or handouts. So, Joe kept his mouth shut for a few days and set out to determine who would help him if they felt he was in need. After soliciting the $100 loans from his friends, Joe had his list.

At his party, Joe lavished gifts upon those who had proven their friendship by loaning him the $100. And he paid back their loans, with interest amounting to several times the original amount borrowed. Joe also pledged to help those friends financially in any way that he could.

As for those fair-weather friends who failed to loan Joe the $100, he developed a stock answer when any of them asked for a loan:

"Uh, well, uh, well, uh, do you think it's going to rain?"

LET THE VOLCANO BLOW

It was about twenty years ago, but I remember it as though it happened yesterday. I was a young upstart, then, and it was the first time I'd ever seen it happen in a business setting. Since then, I've seen it several times with varying results.

Dean and Mike were employees for the same company. They, along with three other people, including myself, were sitting in the coffee room one Friday noon. It was a cordial atmosphere, a few lame jokes and small talk.

Mike was telling about his weekend plans to attend the football game when Dean blew.

"Must be nice to have every weekend off to go partying while the rest of us stay behind and work," Dean said in an accusing tone.

"What do you mean by that smart remark?" Mike snapped.

"I mean some of us do our own job and half of somebody's else's work besides," Dean said with a glare.

"Are you talking about me?" Mike asked firmly.

"If the shoe fits, wear it," Dean said.

"Maybe some of us are just better organized and get our work done on time, while other people don't have what it takes or fool around on the job too much," Mike said with a sneer.

Dean didn't answer. He just lunged across the table and grabbed Mike by the throat. Mike responded by punching Dean in the ribs and on the side of the head. Before either one could cause serious injury, the rest of us got into the act and broke them up.

Somebody insisted that Dean and Mike shake hands, make up, and forget about this little incident. They did, and they didn't. They did shake hands, and they did go through the motions of making up. But they didn't forget about it. This one brief moment of poorly restrained tempers ruined a friendship and working relationship. The company suffered because of it, their co-workers suffered because of it, and, worst of all, they suffered because of it.

I witnessed a similar incident a few years later. Jim and Ron were mid-level executives on the same rung of the corporate ladder. They were both department managers and were both territorial, protecting their own little domains. Their departments had interaction with each other, and, on occasion, controversies occurred. Usually, the controversies were handled smoothly and congenially with a little give-and-take and no long-lasting, hard feelings or territorial wars resulted.

On this one occasion, though, something had apparently gone seriously wrong, and Jim charged into Ron's office. He started yelling and screaming, then he yelled and screamed some more. Jim's face was as red as an apple, and he was so emotionally charged that his entire body was shaking and trembling. In fact, his rear end looked like it was connected to a jackhammer.

Jim aired every complaint he'd ever had with Ron, Ron's department, Ron's employees, the company in general, the assigning of reserved parking spaces, the quality of food in the cafeteria, and, perhaps, the price of tea in China. He recounted how he, and he, alone, had saved the company, how he had worked harder than anyone else over the years, how he cared for the company more than others did, how he had devoted his life to the company, and how nobody appreciated it and how Ron, and everybody else, had just ridden along on his coattails all these years.

Through all this, Ron sat calmly and quietly with his hands folded in his lap. He simply looked at Jim with no emotion whatsoever showing on his face — no anger, no fear, no disgust, no humor, no judgment — nothing. He just sat there.

Finally, after about fifteen minutes, Jim's tirade was over. He stopped yelling and screaming, quit shaking, and his color returned to normal.

After a moment of silence, Ron said in a calm, natural, unaccusing voice, "Are you through?"

Jim was drained, both emotionally and physically. He nodded his head, "Yes."

"Jim," Ron said in a calm, well-controlled voice, "There's a lot of truth in what you say. You have done a lot for the company, and you deserve credit for it."

By this time, Jim had totally cooled down and was more than a little embarrassed by his actions. He was meek as a lamb. He spent the next five minutes explaining how he really hadn't meant some of the things he'd said and spent the following five minutes heaping praise on Ron and his department. Ron and Jim then spent the next ten minutes or so calmly discussing the problem that had originally set Jim off, and they worked out a solution, just as they had done so many times in the past. Then Jim left and neither of them ever mentioned the episode again. But Jim never blew his stack at Ron again, and their working relationship through the following years was actually smoother than ever.

I admired Ron tremendously for the way he had handled the situation, and I still do. He simply sat there and let Jim blow his cork and get the bottled-up frustrations out of his system.

For one thing, Ron knew Jim well enough to realize that this screaming, yelling, shaking maniac wasn't the real Jim and that, after, Jim had said his piece, he'd return to normal. And he did.

For another thing, Ron was self-assured and confident enough of his own abilities and self-worth that he didn't feel the need to defend himself or to attack Jim to get even.

Every now and then someone blows their cork and takes out their momentary frustrations on an innocent, or mostly innocent, bystander. The innocent can react like a Mike from the first story and strike back, or they can react like the Ron from the second story and calmly sit the storm out.

Mike's defend-yourself-and-strike-back solution may be the normal reaction, but it is shortsighted. In the long run, Ron's sit-it-out solution works best. For everyone knows that, after a violent storm passes, there is a period of peaceful calm and tranquility. And, during that calm and tranquility, fences are mended and bridges are repaired, and they often become stronger and more useful than they ever were before the storm.

THE KVASNIKA TECHNIQUE

Although others may have used this technique before him, some may have used it more often, and some may have used it better, no one has ever enjoyed using it more than my friend, Harlan Kvasnika. But, before I divulge *The Kvasnika Technique*, let me give you some background info.

Harlan hates meetings. He considers them to be boring, useless, ineffective, and a waste of time. A group of people get together to discuss a problem that two good people could have solved in fifteen minutes and they foul it up so bad that it requires a series of six or eight more meetings to straighten it out. And it never does get straightened out. You know what they say; a camel is a horse that was designed by a committee.

It's not that Harlan hasn't been to an effective, well run, productive meeting. He has. That was back in 1972, to the best of his recollection.

Harlan told me about one meeting that he was required to attend. The committee consisted of thirty people, which was about twenty-eight too many. The meeting lasted for two hours, and about half of the people there also had to commute an hour, round trip, for the meeting. The sole purpose of the meeting was to try to figure out what the meeting was about, and they never did get the handle on it. Harlan admits that he didn't help things along any, since he spent his time calculating the cost of this meeting. He figured seventy-five hours of time were devoured by this meeting. That's seventy-five hours of people's lives shot. And at an average income of $200 per day per person, this meeting cost the boss $1,875.00 in wages, plus another $198 in auto mileage: a total of $2,073.00.

But it was at this meeting that the seed was sown for what is now widely known as *The Kvasnika Technique*.

About ten minutes into the meeting, a secretary came to the door and beckoned one of the group. Apparently, an important phone call or a visitor required attention. Harlan felt several emotions as he sat there while the other person got up and walked out. First, he was jealous; the other person was leaving, and Harlan was stuck there. Second, Harlan felt inferior. That other person was important enough and irreplaceable enough that he had to be summoned out of the meeting to solve some crisis or handle some big deal. On the other hand, it was apparent that Harlan could be stowed in a meeting for two hours, and the company could still function nicely. The guy never did come back.

About fifteen minutes before the meeting ended, one of the group finally showed up, mumbling something about having important business to attend to and being sorry about missing the meeting. Again, Harlan felt jealous and inferior.

But that was the last meeting Harlan suffered through, for he now uses *The Kvasnika Technique*. He simply "plants" a phone call, or instructs a secretary to summon him from the meeting about ten minutes after it begins. Or, he shows up ten minutes before it ends.

And, others sitting there in the meeting just have to be thinking: "Important guy, that Kvasnika," "Indispensable," "Company can't get along without him," "Important business to attend to," "Irreplaceable." And they are jealous. And they feel inferior. Ahh, the Kvasnika technique.

POTLUCK

It was quite an event at the church. It was looked forward to for the whole year, and tonight was the night — the annual potluck dinner, of course. There was more food there than any army could eat. Hot dishes, cold dishes, salads, breads, cheeses, and deserts of every size, shape, and description. It was all homemade, and it was all wonderful.

The women of the church, and a few men, took great pride in their cooking ability. They delighted in bringing a dish or two to share and got great pleasure from seeing people dig in for a heaping serving. And all around the dining hall you could hear people critiquing the food with glowing compliments.

It was fun to hear someone say something like, "This seven bean salad is simply out of this world — I wonder who made it." And the cook might be sitting right there, silently basking in the wonderful compliment.

That's the good side of a potluck dinner. The side you hear people talking about. The other side, the bad side, people talk about only in whispers, if they talk about it at all. Or, for some people, it's the thought that's in the way far corners of the mind — if it's in their mind at all.

To get right to the point, at a potluck, you never know who stirred what with their feet. Or worse. And, once in a while, somebody brings a dish that is questionable — very questionable. The problem for the kitchen staff, then, is to decide what to do about it. That's exactly what happened at this particular, annual potluck dinner and the whole point of this little story.

The preacher's wife, Mary, was in charge of arranging the dishes on the table. Maybe she volunteered for the job so she could intercept any stirred-with-the-feet-dishes — who knows?

Anyway, as Mary was carrying this one dish to the table, she noticed an odd odor. She took a whiff of the dish, and it almost knocked her over. It smelled sour. Mary was certain it was spoiled. Mary looked at the name on the bottom of the dish — it was a pillar of the church. Apparently she had gotten hold of some spoiled ingredients by accident or had inadvertently let the dish sit out in the heat too long. At any rate, it was spoiled.

Mary knew that, if she served the spoiled dish, it could cause food poisoning for someone who ate it. It could also cause the person who brought it a good deal of embarrassment if people found out that she'd brought a spoiled dish. But Mary didn't want to hurt the cook's feeling by pointing it out to her or sending her home with the full, untouched, dish that hadn't been put out on the food table.

Mary thought about her dilemma for a while and finally came up with a solution.

She discretely put the dish aside in the kitchen when no one was looking. Later, when the others were busy serving the guests, Mary took the dish from its hiding place and dumped the contents down the garbage disposal. Then she put the dish back in its hiding place.

When the dinner was over, Mary placed the dish on the table with the rest of the empty or mostly empty dishes. Therefore when the cook came to claim her dish she'd simply think that she had overlooked it before, and, judging by the empty dish, she'd just naturally assume that it had been a huge hit with the diners.

No one was any the wiser.

BEWARE THE DOOMSAYERS

"Good morning, George!" Bill said, "isn't it a beautiful day!"

"Yea," George replied, "but it's going to rain tomorrow."

The chemistry teacher held up a beaker with red liquid in it, and said, "Class, write down on a piece of paper how much liquid is in this beaker."

Mary wrote, "It's half full."

Jean wrote, "It's half empty."

An industrious couple, Konnie and Kurt, both twenty-eight, had been married for four years and had been saving money for a down payment on a house. When they had accumulated enough money, they went house hunting with a real estate agent. They looked at dozens of houses, town homes, and condos over a four-month period.

Finally, they found exactly what they wanted. It was a two-bedroom, ranch style home with single, attached garage. It was roomy for a two-bedroom and had a fireplace and finished basement. They made an offer on the home, and it was accepted by the seller.

Konnie and Kurt were ecstatic. It was a dream come true. They had planned for this day through four years of marriage and for two years before that. They were jumping up and down and hugging and kissing like a couple of kids. It was a time of great joy.

Konnie and Kurt had not told any of their friends or relatives that they were thinking of buying a house. First, they didn't know if they could actually pull it off, and, second, they wanted to surprise everyone.

Konnie and Kurt were so excited that they just had to tell someone. They had to tell *everyone*. Their first stop was to see their best friends, Mike and Cindy.

"Guess what we just did!" Konnie said. "We bought a house!"

"That's wonderful!" Mike and Cindy said, "But do you think you can afford it?"

Next, Konnie and Kurt told the good news to Kurt's brother, John, and his wife, Carol.

"That's great!" John and Carol said. "But do you think a two-bedroom is big enough — you might have kids some day."

The next stop was at the house of friends Paul and Lynette.

"That's just wonderful! We're so happy for you," Paul and Lynette said, "but I sure wouldn't use that fireplace if I were you — you could get asphyxiated and die in your sleep."

Next, they stopped at the home of Konnie's parents.

"You dumb kids," they said, "by the time you get that $125,000 house paid for it will cost you $300,000 in interest."

The next stop was to see Konnie's sister and her husband.

"That's just great. We're so happy for you," the sister and her husband said. "But, do you think it was wise to buy on South 16th Street? That's a terrible stigma to stick your kids with as they grow up, living on the south side of town."

The final stop was at Jill and Peter's apartment.

"We're happy for you," they said, "but I'd never buy a house in this town. Prices are dropping, and you'll never get your money out of it if you sell."

Konnie and Kurt returned to their apartment. They were glum, sullen, and depressed. All of their joy and excitement were gone. Perhaps without intending to do so, their friends and relatives had, one after the other, planted little seeds of doubt about the home purchase. Or maybe it was jealousy on the part of some and genuine concern on the part of others, but, whatever it was, they had beaten Konnie and Kurt's brains out.

Konnie and Kurt discussed their home purchase that night before they went to bed. Could they afford it? Was the house big enough? Would it cost too much in the long run? Would the address be an embarrassment to them and to their children, if they ever had any? Could they ever sell it if they wanted to?

They awoke the next morning in a panic, bordering on hysteria. Buying the house had been a terrible mistake. The house was too small and in a bad location and the fireplace was a silent time bomb. And, they were paying too much for it and could never sell it if they wanted to some day.

Konnie and Kurt called their real estate agent. They had to see him right away, even if it was Sunday morning.

The agent met Konnie and Kurt at the real estate office, and they explained that they had made a horrible mistake and wanted out of the deal. Even if they had to forfeit the $1,000 earnest money payment they had made, they wanted out.

They then went on to detail the long list of reasons they had for wanting to call the deal off. The agent said he understood their having second thoughts — it was called "post-purchase dissonance" or, "buyer's remorse." Everybody gets it, he explained.

The agent suggested that they go take one last look at the home before Konnie and Kurt made a final decision to cancel the deal.

When they arrived at the house with the real estate agent, Konnie and Kurt were surprised. The neighborhood wasn't a slum; it was pretty nice. And the home was attractive and roomy and homey. And the fireplace operated on natural gas and was totally harmless. In fact, everything was exactly as they had remembered it the day before. Maybe better.

And they analyzed their finances and the house payments and, yes, they could afford it. And, the real estate agent showed them example after example of how homes in that neighborhood had increased in value and of how owners had sold them at a profit, not a loss.

Konnie and Kurt went ahead with the deal as planned, moved in, and still live there today. They've never missed a house payment, and the home has increased in value by $30,000.

Yes, the world is full of doomsayers who can find no good in any situation or, perhaps, who just can't stand to see others happy and successful. Or, maybe, they don't even know that they're sending out negative vibes.

Whatever the reason, beware the doomsayers. They will surface when you may least expect them and predict doom, gloom, and despair. But do your own thinking, and stick to what you believe is right. You shall overcome the doomsayers and do just fine.

THE MCNUTT TECHNIQUE

I could have called it *Uncle Fred's Technique*, since he was the first I ever saw use it, or *Peter Davidson's Technique*, since I've used it often. But I'll call it *The McNutt Technique*, because that's what I normally call it. It's named after my friend, Dan McNutt. Others may have used it first, and some may have used it more often; but none have used it better. Dan McNutt is a master of *The McNutt Technique*.

Here's the scoop. Every year there are, at least, a half dozen, if not a full dozen, events that a person is required to go to by one's employer, spouse, or sense of duty. These include graduations, weddings, recitals, and stuff like that.

They're a waste of time. Right? Your being there or not being there doesn't really make a difference — the event will come off, anyway. Right? And you hate going and are miserable when you're there. Right? But you know you have to go, so you do go. And you waste your time, and you suffer.

But it doesn't have to be this way. You can go but not be there. You can use *The McNutt Technique*.

Here's how it works. At any of these events there's a time just before the event or just after the event when everybody is milling around, shaking hands and saying "Hi." This is when you are highly visible. During the event, itself, you sit down some place in a corner, and nobody notices you because the focus is on the event.

With *The McNutt Technique* you are there — but only during the highly visible period. You slip out just as the event is to begin or show up right after it's over. Everybody knows you were there, and they're happy. But you really weren't there, and you're happy.

Right now, at the very moment I am writing these words, I'm at a graduation exercise. At least 200 people who know me have seen me and will swear to it. Dan McNutt is at the same graduation.

The ceremony will be over in about forty-five minutes, so I've got to go. McNutt is waiting for me in the car.

VII.
THE SWEETEST REVENGE

Tit for tat. Getting even. Sometimes there's nothing sweeter. And if we're going to get even, we may as well do it with style and class — and even have a few laughs along the way.

It is better to die on your feet than to live on your knees. Delores Ibarruri

It's useless to hold a person to anything he says while he's in love, drunk, or running for office. Shirley MacLaine

If thine enemy offend thee, give his child a drum. Anonymous

Conscience is a mother-in-law whose visit never ends. H. L. Mencken

Nearly all men can stand adversity, but if you want to test a man's character, give him power. Abraham Lincoln

To be vain of one's rank or place is to show that one is below it. Staniscas I

Time wounds all heels. Anonymous

It's not the size of the dog in the fight, it's the size of the fight in the dog. Mark Twain

There are some defeats more triumphant than victories. Michel de Montaigne

The best manner of avenging ourselves is by not resembling him who had injured us. Jane Porter

There is no revenge so complete as forgiveness. Josh Billings

Forgive your enemies, but never forget their names. John F. Kennedy

MR. PONY TAIL

The seasoned salesmen all agreed — he didn't look like much. Maybe thirty years old, wrinkled T-shirt, faded jeans, thinning hair pulled back in a pony tail. Wandering around out there in the car lot carrying a suitcase, looking at the new Caddys, checking the price tags.

The old pros had seen guys like him before — tire kickers. No need to even go out and talk to him — a waste of time. Besides that, it was hot and almost closing time. So, the salesmen continued to tell each other a few jokes as they watched the pony-tailed tire kicker drool over the new Cadillacs. Once in a while, Mr. Pony Tail would glance in at the office, but they weren't going to fall for that old ploy.

After he'd kicked the tires on every one of those Caddys, Mr. Pony Tail headed for the office. He walked in, set his suitcase down inside the door, and walked over to the group of salesmen who had been watching him.

"I'd like to talk to your youngest, least experienced salesperson," he said.

"That would be Jim," one of them said, pointing to a young man busily sorting through some papers on his desk.

"I'd like to take that green Eldorado for a test drive," Mr. Pony Tail said.

Jim jumped up, shook hands with Mr. Pony Tail, introduced himself, and grabbed the keys to the car.

Jim suggested that he start out driving so Mr. Pony Tail could get a feel for the car before taking the wheel. That was fine with Mr. Pony Tail.

Jim had driven only about two miles and was only about halfway through his presentation when Mr. Pony Tail interrupted him.

"I'll take it," he said, "on one condition. You've got to drive me to my destination — it's about 100 miles from here. I'll get you back."

Of course, Jim agreed, and Mr. Pony Tail wrote him a check for the full amount on the spot.

Jim found Mr. Pony Tail to be wonderful company on their 100 mile drive, although he was a little mysterious.

When they reached Mr. Pony Tail's destination, a large factory, he got out and shook Jim's hand. Jim handed Mr. Pony Tail the keys, but Mr. Pony Tail held up the palms of his hands to refuse them.

"The car's yours," Mr. Pony Tail said. "Now go back to your dealership, and tell your bosses not to judge a book by its cover."

You see, Mr. Pony Tail was looking at cars that day for one reason. He had flown into the city and thought it would be less of a hassle to buy a car than to rent one for his 100 mile journey. For, you see, Mr. Pony Tail in his wrinkled T-shirt and faded blue jeans was founder, CEO, and major stockholder in one of the fastest-growing telecommunication companies in the world — one of the richest men in the world, worth billions.

And Mr. Pony Tail was right, you can't always judge a book by its cover or, in this case, a man by his pony tail.

WELCOME ABOARD, MATE

Anne worked in the accounting department. Bill was the new guy in personnel. Anne was single. Bill was in the process of getting a divorce.

They met the third day Bill was on the job. He was anxious to make new friends. She was helpful in showing him the ropes.

Bill had moved from another city about 150 miles away and had leased a small apartment. After his divorce was final, Bill would find a larger apartment or buy a house. Bill went home on weekends to visit his two children.

After Bill had been on the job about two weeks, he asked Anne to lunch. It was mostly shop talk and small talk. Bill said it felt strange, but good, being out with another woman after twelve years of marriage.

The tempo increased. Bill and Anne went out once a week, sometimes twice. Dinner, a movie, cocktails, dancing — it was a good time. But they kept their relationship low-key around the office, since office romances were frowned on by the boss. The boss felt office lovers would spend all day writing love letters instead of writing contracts. So, at work, Bill and Anne barely acknowledged each other.

Anne moved into a new apartment, and Bill helped. He bought her a beautiful, framed art reproduction to hang above her sofa. Anne treasured the gift.

One day, Anne had lunch with a friend who worked in the personnel department as a secretary. She particularly liked working with the new guy, Bill, she volunteered. What a wonderful guy, so hard working and so competent. Anne was inwardly pleased, her assessment exactly, but she showed little outward interest.

The secretary continued. That Bill, such a devoted family man. Why, he called his wife at least once a day, and he often sent her flowers or candy. He just couldn't wait to get home to his wife and kids on weekends. As soon as they sold their house, the family would move here, but until then Bill was renting a small apartment.

Anne could feel the emotions rise within her. Thank God she hadn't fallen in love with the jerk — she was starting to slip, but she hadn't fallen. She was mad. But, mostly, she felt betrayed and used. Fortunately, it was Friday, and she wouldn't have to face him again until Monday. And then she would tell him off in no uncertain terms, the creep. She had the whole weekend to choose her words very carefully.

On Saturday afternoon, Anne was running some errands, and her route took her right past Bill's apartment. And there was Bill! With a woman — his wife, no doubt. Bill kissed her good-bye and got into his car, apparently to run a few errands of his own.

Anne rushed back to her home. She returned to Bill's apartment, and his car was parked out front. Anne walked boldly up to the door and rang the bell. Bill's wife answered the door. An attractive, nice woman.

"Mrs. Anders?" Anne asked politely.

"Yes," she replied, a little confused.

"I'm Anne Wilson. I work with your husband. Is he here?"

Mrs. Anders led Anne to the kitchen. Bill almost fell through the floor when his wife and girlfriend walked into the room together.

"Thank you for loaning me this beautiful art reproduction," Anne said as she handed it to Bill, "But I won't be needing it, anymore. Well, I must be going. So nice to meet you, Mrs. Anders. Good-bye."

Bill had some tall explaining to do — like "Where did that painting come from, and why did you loan it to her?" "Why are you shaking?" "Why are you so pale all of a sudden?" and "Who the hell was that woman?"

Anne got her revenge, perhaps in double. And, she did it without lowering herself to Bill's level. And, yes, this is one of those true stories.

OLD TIME ROCK 'N' ROLL

They were good. Even though they were only a local band made up of local guys, they were good. It wasn't long before their reputation spread. They became a regional sensation and then a statewide phenomenon, and eventually they played all over the country. Not bad for a bunch of guys in their early twenties.

The guys in the band were all good musicians, and the lead singer was great. Somewhere about halfway through the band's three-year life, the lead singer got to thinking that he was more valuable than any of the other members. Being more valuable, he reasoned, he was entitled to a double cut on payday.

He approached the rest of the band with his request, and it was poorly received. Damn poorly.

The lead singer exploded, "I'm the star of the show. Without me, you guys would be nothing." Stuff like that.

Still, the matter was unresolved.

The next night, the band played a gig in Memphis. As usual, the rest of the band started out with two songs while the lead singer waited in the wings, to kind of warm up the crowd. Then the lead singer was called out, and the concert began. On this night, the lead singer was introduced in highly complimentary, flowery terms.

"Ladies and gentlemen, we'd like to introduce the star of our show, Barry Reed. Without Barry, this band would be nothing. Barry makes this band what it is. We all owe a lot to Barry. We owe *everything* to Barry. Let's here it for B-A-A-A-R-R-R-E-E-E R-E-E-E-E-E-D."

The crowd went wild. Barry must have been pleased.

The order of songs for every concert was the same. Barry's first song was always "Runaway," which was a big hit for Del Shannon. It was a difficult song to sing since it covers about two and a half octaves and a few of the high notes are in the glass-shattering range. Most singers wouldn't tackle the song early in the concert, because they'd want to warm up their voice first. But Barry always warmed up backstage and liked to start with "Runaway" since it showcased the power and range of his voice so well.

Barry took the stage like a whirlwind, and the band launched into "Runaway" — one octave higher than normal.

After hearing the first three notes, Barry knew he was screwed. After that great intro, the fans thought he was the greatest singer in the world. He couldn't walk off the stage, and he couldn't stop the band and have them start over — they probably wouldn't stop, anyway. So, he had to sing the song.

Notes that were normally in mid-range were now in the glass-shattering range and those that were normally in the glass-shattering range were now undetectable to the human ear. Barry reached for everything within him for those high notes and thought his vocal cords were going to snap. Barry made it through the song, but it wasn't pretty.

Funny, but Barry kind of forgot about that pay raise he requested after singing that memorable version of "Runaway."

THE MAKEUP EXAM

Professor Barrett had a firm policy — miss the final exam, and I'll see you next semester. No leeway. No slack. No excuses. You flunk. Adios.

Two of Professor Barrett's students, Cal and Ernie, went to visit friends in another college town about 150 miles away on the weekend prior to final exams. Their plan was to return home on Sunday evening so they could study a little before Professor Barrett's final exam at 8:00 Monday morning.

Cal and Ernie had such a great time with their friends that they modified their plans slightly. They would party with their friends on Sunday, go to bed early Sunday night, get up early Monday morning, study for the exam during the drive home, and arrive well ahead of Professor Barrett's 8:00 exam. No problem.

Well, the problem was that Cal and Ernie blew it. They partied way too late, got to bed way too late, and didn't wake up until 8:00 A.M. — the precise moment they were to be taking Professor Barrett's exam.

Cal and Ernie knew that Professor Barrett would never let them take the final exam if they told him the truth. So, they decided to do the only logical thing — they would fabricate a story that Professor Barrett might sympathize with and, therefore, let them take the final exam, after all. Nothing too far-fetched like being kidnapped by aliens, but a nice little, simple, believable lie.

Cal and Ernie arrived on campus about 11:30 A.M. and immediately sought out Professor Barrett. The Professor listened intently to their story about how they had gone away for the weekend to study with friends at that other university, where, coincidentally, their friends were taking the same course as they were taking from Professor Barrett. They had studied late into the night Sunday but had, nevertheless, risen at 4:45 A.M. for the return trip home.

All was going well until they were out in the middle of nowhere at about 5:30 A.M. when, all of a sudden, they blew a tire. Much to their dismay, there was no spare tire. It took until about 8:00 A.M. before they could find a service station open to fix the tire. And then they had hustled back to campus and came straight to Professor Barrett.

They knew the policy about missing the final exam, they explained, but hoped that the Professor could show some lenience since they would have arrived on time had it not been for the flat tire — an event wholly out of their control.

Professor Barrett said he understood their dilemma and, yes, they could take the exam that afternoon at 2:00 P.M.

Cal and Ernie congratulated themselves on the sales job they had done on Professor Barrett. And they actually used the time until shortly before 2:00 P.M. to study for the test.

Professor Barrett explained to Cal and Ernie that their answers to the final exam could very well determine their grades in the course.

The professor explained that he would be in his office if either of them had any questions and that they should bring their completed tests to him. Then he put each of them in a separate room to take the exam.

Things were going perfectly for Cal and Ernie. Perfectly until they opened the test booklet and found that it contained only one short question.

"Which tire?"

"HEY, BABY, DO YOU WANNA..."

For a woman, receiving an obscene phone call can be disgusting. Receiving a second obscene call can be worrisome, and receiving continued obscene phone calls can be unnerving.

Characteristically, when a woman gets an obscene phone call, she is appalled, disgusted, worried, and scared. "Who is it?" "How did they get my phone number?" "What do they want?" "Are they going to continue pestering me?" "Will they stalk me?" "Do they intend to rape me?" "Murder me?"

These are normal, human reactions and concerns. If my wife, daughter, sister, or friend received an obscene phone call, I'd share these same concerns with them.

The typical obscene phone call starts with some heavy breathing followed by a barrage of smutty suggestions and insults.

Typically, the recipient of the call says, "Who is this?" and then slams the receiver down. Or the recipient may tell them off and slam the receiver. Undoubtedly, this is what the caller expects and, most likely, wants. They have scared the hell out of somebody. They have got them on the run.

My friend, Sharon, received an obscene phone call. It was the typical obscene phone call starting with the heavy breathing followed by, "Hey, Baby, do you want to get together and... " Well, all sorts of things.

Now, Sharon is a brassy, self-fulfilled, strong-willed type of person. She didn't scream, tell him off, or slam down the receiver.

"Hey, sugar, you sound like my kind of guy," she began in sexy voice, "Why don't we get together some time. Maybe we could meet somewhere."

Sharon was still talking when *he* slammed down the receiver. Maybe he smelled a cop or a trap — whatever it was, he never called back.

THE TEST

I was teaching a college course in accounting. It was mid-semester, and I gave the second exam of the term.

I had a free period after accounting class and sat down to check the tests immediately. I was always anxious to see how the students did. It was a measure of their ability, and of mine. It was a three page test and I checked everyone's page one first, then everyone's page two, and then everyone's page three. Then, I went back and added up the scores. This was always interesting, since I knew there were some good test papers and some horrible ones, but I didn't know who had done what until this point.

It was a 100 point test. Jeanne had 89; Bill, 76; Anne, 90; Calvin, 64; Bob, 82; Phyllis, 94; Jim, 57; Bernard, 96... .

"Bernard, ninety-six?" I said, aloud in disbelief, "Bernard, ninety-six?"

I paged through Bernard's test and added the points again. It was ninety-six. I got out my answer key and checked the paper again, slowly, carefully. It was ninety-six.

I grabbed my grade book and checked. I was right; Bernard had gotten thirty-eight on the first test. And since the first test, Bernard had handed in no assignments, had cut class four times, and had pretty much slept through class when he was there. I had called on Bernard several times, and he couldn't answer even the simplest questions. And now he got ninety-six on the test. On my test.

"That S.O.B.," I muttered. Bernard had cheated on the test. There was no doubt about it. But, unless you *catch* a student cheating, you can't do anything about it. And I hadn't caught Bernard. I would have to give him the ninety-six.

I was sick. It wasn't fair to the other students who studied for the test and earned the scores they got. It wasn't fair to me to have to give Bernard a grade he didn't earn. It wasn't even fair to Bernard for him to go through life thinking the reason for taking a college course is to get a grade, any way you can, rather than to learn something. But mostly I was mad. I was mad that I had been had. I didn't know how he did it, but Bernard did a number on me.

I thought back and recounted the test period. Bernard had sat in his normal chair, third row on the left. Sally sat in front of him, and Jim was to his left. They had both bombed the test so bad that Bernard couldn't have copied from them. And a crib sheet — well,

Bernard could have the damn book in front of him, and he still couldn't figure this stuff out. And it was a brand new test that I had concocted and duplicated on Friday. So there were no copies floating around campus from previous semesters. Yes, Bernard had really done a number on me. But, how? How did he do it?

In addition to my problem with Bernard, I was perturbed that there had been a mouse in my office over the weekend. When I had entered my office in the morning, I had immediately noticed the white particles on the floor by the stack of papers along the wall. Apparently, a mouse had chewed up some of the papers. I didn't like mice, and I was afraid the mouse was still in my office.

What a way to start the week, under attack from Bernard, and a mouse.

I was sitting there, gazing at the wall, trying to figure out how Bernard had cheated, when my eyes noticed a couple of smudges on the wall and then something that looked like a hand print. My eyes drifted up to the ceiling, then down to the particles of paper the mouse had chewed up, and then quickly back to the ceiling. One of the two-foot-square ceiling tiles wasn't resting on the metal bracket quite right. It was raised up a little bit. Funny I'd never noticed that before.

In a flash I had it. I knew exactly how Bernard had cheated.

Bernard had gotten into the building over the weekend. Although it was locked, students sometimes came in through the hatch in the roof. He had crawled through a ceiling tile in the hallway, gotten on top of the cement block wall, and walked along it above the ceiling until he came to my office. When he got to my office, he pulled up the ceiling tile and lowered himself. But that stack of papers about two feet high was on the floor along the wall, so Bernard had used his foot and hand to shove off from the wall so he didn't land on the papers. And the paper particles from the mouse, they were particles that had scraped off the ceiling tile when Bernard had lifted it up from its metal frame.

Then, Bernard had found the test, which was in plain view on a shelf behind my desk. He sat down in my chair, at my desk, and copied the answers from my answer key onto a blank test paper. Then he straightened things out and walked out of my door, through the reception area, into the hallway, and out of the building. He handed that paper in during the test period.

I felt great; I had figured it out. I felt like Sherlock Holmes at his best. And I was relieved that there hadn't been a mouse in my office, after all.

But then I came back to reality. I now knew exactly how Bernard had cheated, but I couldn't do anything about it. I knew I was right, but all my evidence was circumstantial. I couldn't accuse Bernard, and I couldn't even ask him about it. All he would have to do is deny it. And, he would deny it.

There. You now have all the facts in this case. Before reading any further, why don't you develop a solution. How would you handle it?

As I said, in the first chapter of this book, the solution isn't always so obvious and may not come quickly, but there is an acceptable solution. Somewhere.

It took me about three hours, but a solution was beginning to take shape. Then, finally, all the pieces came together. I smiled to myself. And I laughed out loud. Now, if I could only pull it off.

The accounting class met three days a week, on Monday, Wednesday, and Friday. I gave the test on Monday, so Wednesday was the day to hand back the test and to review it in class.

I walked into class on Wednesday and took my place at the lectern. I looked straight at Bernard and said, "Bernard, will you come with me, please."

He got up and followed me. We walked to my office in silence. I sat down behind my desk, in the authority position. Bernard sat on the chair facing me.

"I want to talk to you about your test," I said in a firm, unemotional unaccusing tone. I thought perhaps Bernard would crack and confess, but no such luck. He didn't flinch. He didn't answer. He sat there calmly and waited for me to continue. He was good.

"Did you turn your test paper in on Monday?" I asked.

Bernard looked puzzled, "What do you mean?" he asked calmly.

"Well, I don't have a test paper from you," I said. "I'm very puzzled by it all, because I know you took the test. You didn't, by chance, turn in your scratch paper and throw your test paper in the waste basket, did you?"

Bernard's eyes rolled a little, and he was getting a little testy. "I *know* I turned the paper in," he said, "and I *know* I did good on the test, too."

"Well, I thought you probably did turn your test paper in, Bernard, I just wanted to check every possibility of what might have happened," I explained.

"But I believe I do know what happened to your test paper, Bernard. This may sound far-fetched, but someone broke into my office last night," I said, referring to Tuesday night. I paused for a moment to let it sink in.

I could sense Bernard wanted to scream, "That was Sunday night, you dummy," but he couldn't.

"They crawled through a ceiling tile in the hallway, walked along the cement block wall above the ceiling, and came down into my office through that ceiling tile right there," I continued, pointing to the ceiling as I reconstructed every move Bernard had made.

Bernard was getting tense. He slumped back in his chair.

I was on a roll, and I continued, pointing everything out to Bernard as I spoke. "You can see here where they pushed off from the wall with their feet and hand to avoid that stack of papers on the floor. And see these particles on the floor, they were scraped from that ceiling tile."

Bernard slumped a little more.

"Now here's the strange part, Bernard," I continued. "The only thing I can find missing from my office is *your test*. Someone broke in here and stole your test paper."

Bernard looked like he had been hit in the face with a shovel. I had him. And he knew I had him. And he knew there wasn't a damn thing he could do about it. It was one of my finest hours.

"Now I do need a test from you, Bernard," I explained, "So you'll have to take it again. It should be even easier the second time since you've already seen the test. I'm sure you'll do just as well as you did the first time."

I sat Bernard down at a desk in the reception area and left him under the watchful eye of a colleague, while I returned to accounting class to review the test.

This time, Bernard got thirty-six on the test. Justice was served.

FILLERUP

My friend, Norm, went to his Uncle Harvey's funeral near Boston. During the service, someone got up and recalled a humorous incident from Harvey's life. Then another got up and another and another. Finally, after two hours of humorous, tender, and outrageous "Harvey stories," the pastor had to put an end to it, because another funeral was scheduled to begin in a short time. Those who knew Harvey well said the stories could have continued on for several more hours.

Harvey owned a gas station near the university, and it seemed that, at one time or another, nearly everyone in the community and almost every college student had worked for Harvey.

One such college student, Brandon, worked for Harvey part-time during his last three years of college. On the day he graduated with his degree in engineering, Brandon stopped in to get his final paycheck and to bid Harvey and his gas station goodbye.

It was a big day for Brandon, and he was feeling like he could whip the world. In fact, you might say he was a little cocky, since he's already landed a job with an engineering firm in the community — quite a step up from pumping gas.

Brandon shook Harvey's hand as he pocketed his final paycheck and said with a touch of superiority and arrogance in his voice, "I'll never pump gas for you, again."

Seventeen years later, Brandon's sixteen-year-old son, Evan, was looking for his first part-time job. Naturally, Brandon thought of Harvey right off. Brandon took Evan to apply for the job, and Harvey said, "You bet I can use Evan; have him here at 6:30, sharp, tomorrow morning."

At 6:25 A.M., Brandon and Evan arrived at Harvey's gas station. It was completely dark. They walked around the outside of the station — no one in sight. They peered through the window of the office — the lights were off, and nobody was inside. Brandon tried the door — it was open.

Brandon and Evan cautiously entered the gas station, not knowing what to expect. There on the counter was a note to Evan and a whole list of things he was to do to open the station, turn the pumps on, and get everything going.

At that moment, a car pulled up to the pump for gas. Since Evan was inexperienced, Brandon instinctively rushed out to the pump to serve the customer.

Brandon had just begun pumping gas when he heard this loud laughter. He looked around and finally located its source. There was Harvey up on the roof of the gas station.

"I though you said you'd never pump gas for me again!" Harvey yelled. And then he cut loose with one of those "He who laughs last laughs best" laughs that had been stored up for seventeen years.

I wish I'd have known Harvey. Sounds like he was quite a guy.

THE CONDO COMMANDMENT

If you already know what a condominium is and how it operates, you can skip this first paragraph, and go to paragraph two. A condominium is a form of home ownership where each resident of an apartment building owns their own apartment. And each condo owner owns a share of the *common elements*, which include things like the roof, hallways, grounds, parking lot, and swimming pool that are used by everyone. Each condo owner can do whatever they want with the interior of their unit, but no one can do anything to the exterior of the building, or the common elements, without a majority vote of the condo owners.

I've researched this carefully. You can ask anyone who has ever lived in a condo, and they'll verify it as fact. In any condo, there is one guy who questions every move made by the president and condo association board. He writes letters to the president, the board, and the other condo owners. He drafts petitions. He makes phone calls. He calls unauthorized meetings. He forms groups. He talks to the zoning commission, the utility company, the city, the county, and the state to try to get rates and regulations changed. He creates havoc at meetings. He thinks that every motion is unconstitutional. He wants a recount of the vote. He wants a committee formed to study the constitution. He wants to re-write the by-laws.

This guy is called the *Condo Commando*.

In the condo where Shelly lives, there are only twenty-four units, but they, too, have their Condo Commando. He operates exactly like every other Condo Commando at every other condo.

A group of owners in the building asked if she would accept the nomination for president of the condo association. She was flattered, but declined. She told them she didn't want to spend the next year of her life under siege from the Condo Commando. When she asked if one of them would take the presidency, they all declined for the same reason — the Condo Commando.

Shelly had a solution in mind, though, and they agreed it was worth a try. They elected the Condo Commando president. Now the shoe's on the other foot. By nature of the office, the Condo Commando must follow the rules. And now he is under attack from the other twenty-three condo owners, who are really enjoying being Condo Commandos.

YOU MAY PASS THIS WAY AGAIN

I recently saw an entertaining television commercial encouraging people to play the state lottery. A woman wearing an old-fashioned dress, square-heeled shoes, and a pillbox hat is walking down a long, empty hallway in an office building. She opens every door, sticks her head in, and screams, "I won."

When she gets to the boss' office at the end of the hall, she opens the door, sticks her tongue out, flutters her lips, and yells, "I quit."

No doubt every person alive has daydreamed, at one time or another, of similarly telling off the boss, a customer, a neighbor, a relative, or someone else, especially if we knew we'd never have to see them again.

There are lots of little instances in life where someone has flubbed up and where we could really lambaste them if we wanted to, and nobody would blame us.

But even in these situations where we have the upper hand, and, seemingly, have nothing to lose by venting our hostility or frustration at someone else's expense, the best policy is still to use tact and finesse instead of a sledgehammer. You see, these circumstances may be only temporary, and you may need to pass this way again someday. And when you do, there could be hell to pay.

I recall, for instance, the time a couple of years ago when my wife and I had planned a trip to New York City. We booked the flight four months in advance.

About a week before our departure, my wife was going to be out of town for a few days and gave me strict instructions to make sure to pick up our tickets from the travel agency.

I stopped at the travel agency to get the tickets, and the agent didn't have them. We had already picked them up, she said. In fact, the agent distinctly recalled my wife stopping in to pay for the tickets and remembered giving the tickets to her at that time. That was several weeks ago, she said.

I returned home and checked the wall safe where we would ordinarily put such airline tickets for safekeeping — no tickets. I called my wife, reminded her that she had already picked up the tickets, and asked if she remembered where she had put them. She had absolutely no recollection of ever picking up the tickets.

"How could anyone go to a travel agency just a few weeks ago, pay them hundreds of dollars, receive the tickets, and not remember a thing about it? How could anybody be so stupid!" I screamed in disbelief. But I said this to myself — not out loud to my wife.

I prodded her to look in that portable storage shed she refers to as a purse. She was reluctant to do so, being convinced that she didn't have the tickets and, also realizing that hunting through her purse was a major project. Finally, she looked — no tickets.

This time I said it out loud, but I didn't scream and I didn't yell and I didn't accuse. It took some self-control.

"Think back, do you remember being in the travel agency?"

"No," she said.

"Do you remember writing a check for the tickets or putting them on a credit card?"

"No," she said.

"Well, do you remember driving the car into the travel agency parking lot or parking the car or anything at all?"

"No."

"Well, did the agent give you any travel brochures or fun books or maps or anything?" I asked, trying to jog her memory.

"No," she replied, "I don't remember anything."

"You mean you can't remember driving to the travel agency, getting out of the car, walking into the agency, paying for the tickets, taking the tickets from the travel agent's hand, walking out of the travel agency, getting back into the car — nothing?"

"No," she replied again; she remembered nothing.

I promised to hunt through every drawer and hiding place in the house and to call her back in an hour. I hung up the phone and hung my head in disbelief. That woman's lack of memory was going to ruin this trip that we'd been planning for months.

"How," I said out loud, "Could this woman not remember a thing? How?"

I was about halfway through my search of every hiding place we'd ever used when the phone rang. It was my wife.

"I finally remembered about going to the travel agency," she said.

"Well, it's about time," I said smugly. But, again, I said this to myself, not to her.

"What I remember," she said, "is that you went to the travel agency — not me."

"Me?" I said in disbelief, "Me?"

"Don't you remember," she said, "You were going to drive right past there that day you were going to get fertilizer for the lawn, and you stopped in along the way."

I vaguely recalled something about it, but it was pretty hazy.

"Think back, do you remember being in the travel agency office?" she asked.

"No," I said.

"Do you remember writing a check for the ticket or putting them on a credit card?"

"No," I said.

"Well, do you remember driving the car into the travel agency parking lot or parking the car or anything at all?"

"No," I said, responding to a series of questions that sounded very familiar. She had a better memory than I thought.

"Well, did the agent give you any travel brochures or fun books or maps or anything?" she asked.

"No," I said, "I don't remember anything."

"You mean you can't remember driving to the travel agency, getting out of the car, walking into the agency, paying for the tickets, taking the tickets from the travel agent's hand, walking out of the travel agency, getting back into the car — nothing?"

"No," I replied, again — I remembered nothing.

I imagine my wife was pretty upset with me for not being able to remember a thing about picking up the tickets. She was probably shaking her head in disgust and cursing me under her breath, but she didn't let it show. In all fairness, she had to treat me nice, for when the situation was reversed, I had treated her nice. Thank God, I had.

I was about to resume my search for the missing tickets when the phone rang. It was the travel agent. She had found our tickets in their safe. Apparently, she said, it was someone else she was thinking of who had picked up tickets a few weeks ago — not my wife. She had my check for the tickets, too — I had mailed it to her.

Now I remembered. I was supposed to stop to pay for the tickets about two months ago when I went to buy lawn fertilizer, but there was a sale on fertilizer at another store than the one I'd planned to go to. I never did get in the vicinity of the travel agency. So, I mailed a check the next day and enclosed a note saying we'd pick up the tickets a week or so before our trip.

When the travel agent told me she had been mistaken about having given us the tickets, I felt like blowing my top for a brief moment, but I didn't. I was nice to her, for a couple of reasons. First of all, being nice is the right thing to do. Secondly, I may do business with her again, and I'll want her to think kindly of me and put forth her best effort, rather than being mad at me or vindictive.

I recall another situation where someone had the upper hand and could have mistreated an underling if they had been so inclined, but it paid for them to be nice. My friend, Oscar, was a district manager for his company. When Oscar's boss' boss retired as regional manager, the company didn't move Oscar's boss up to that position, they moved Oscar up. Leapfrogging, they call it. Now, all of a sudden, Oscar was boss over his former boss. I'll bet that Oscar's former boss was thankful that he had always treated Oscar respectfully and kindly, or, surely, the rest of his career with the company would not only have been miserable, but also short.

Yes, even if you have the upper hand and could grind someone under your thumb, it pays to use tact and finesse and to be nice, for, surely, you may pass this way again.

Oh, yes, my wife and I went to the travel agent to get our tickets, together, and we had a wonderful time in New York City.

A STUDENT

Andy Anderson was a college student, using the term loosely, who was variously described by his professors as a "Slacker," "Rummy," "Dum Dum," and "Yo Yo." Oh, Andy was a good enough guy — everybody liked him — but he wasn't much of a student. Apparently, Andy had successfully navigated high school on his likable nature, boyish charm, and twenty-three-point-a-game average — and, perhaps, the ready assistance of a bevy of eager, young ladies.

In college, Andy was prone to cutting classes, handing in assignments late, if at all, and bombing tests. All of this was usually followed by end-of-the-semester repentance and begging for a grade — any grade. Sometimes it worked.

Andy found himself in his normal position at the end of the semester in Professor Abbott's sociology class. The final course grade was to be determined by test scores (60%), attendance (10%), and a term paper (30%). Andy was in tough shape in the tests and attendance, so the term paper, due at the end of the semester, was his only hope. In fact, Professor Abbott had tried to inspire Andy to give the paper a serious effort by telling him an above average paper could earn Andy a D for a final course grade; a superior paper might even raise Andy's grade to a C.

On the final day that the term paper could be handed in, five minutes after the official 4:00 P.M. deadline, of course, Andy delivered his term paper to Professor Abbott. And it was obvious that Andy was proud of the manuscript.

Professor Abbott paged through the term paper. It was a masterpiece — headings, subheadings, footnotes, quotations, charts, graphs, a bibliography — you name it. The seasoned Professor Abbott was suspicious.

"This is impressive," Professor Abbott said.

Andy beamed.

Professor Abbott turned the term paper face down on his desk and calmly asked, "What's the title of your term paper, Andy?"

Andy's face went blank.

Professor Abbott pressed on, "Tell me the title of your term paper, and I'll give you an A on it."

Andy gulped. His eyes rolled. His heart sunk, and so did his grade.

CUT TO THE QUICK

The reason I know this works is that I've had people do it to me. And, at the time, it cut me to the quick. Let me tell you a couple of stories.

This guy, Dan, was a tinkerer. Eventually, after tinkering around for a couple of years, he invented some equipment that you can attach to your lawn mower, and he made millions. He's a cool guy who appreciates his success and who — Well, he acts pretty normal. Mike and Dan aren't fast friends, but Mike knows Dan well enough to stop and visit for a while when he meets him on the street.

Mike had met Dan's wife, Jean, a couple of times over the past year or two and had even had a couple of short conversations with her. You might say that she revels in Dan's success a little more than he does. Anyway, let's say Mike knows Jean well enough to say hello by name when he meets her on the street.

That's why Mike was rather stunned when he and his wife and another couple met Dan and Jean at a party last summer.

"Do you know Dan and Jean?" their friend asked, making introductions.

"Of course I know Mike," Dan said as he shook his hand.

"No," Jean said, studying Mike for a moment, "I don't think we've ever met."

And then she shot her hand straight out, stiff as a board, in her best "I'm the boss' wife" handshake.

"Never met?" Mike said to himself, "Never met?"

Mike wanted to explain, "Don't you recall the time we met at the Olson's party or the time we talked about great American poets at the Ivy Restaurant or the time we met when you were with our mutual friends, the Harveys?"

But Mike shook that stiff hand of hers and let it lie.

But, Mike said he'd never forget that deflated feeling. That feeling of not counting — of not being important enough for her to remember his name. Mike didn't know if she did it on purpose or not, but she did it.

And he didn't forget it.

About two months later, Mike was at another party and he bumped into Dan and Jean. This time he was ready.

"Dan and Jean, do you know Mike?" the host asked.

"Hello, Mike," Dan said as they shook hands.

Jean shot her stiff as a board hand out for a handshake.

"Um," Mike said, momentarily eyeing Jean, "I don't think we've ever met. I'm Mike Anders."

Jean's mouth dropped open, and a bewildered look of disbelief settled in.

"I, uh, we, uh, we met at the Hagan party a couple of months ago, and we've met a time or two before that," Jean explained.

Mike imagined her mind doing cartwheels, saying things like "How could that idiot forget meeting *me*?" "Doesn't he know who I am?" "How could he forget *my* name?" "Do I count so little?" "Am I not important enough to be remembered?"

Mike reached out and shook Jean's hand. It had turned to mush.

"I don't recall," Mike lied, "But, it's nice seeing you again."

Mike met Dan and Jean at a restaurant about a month after that party. He walked up and greeted them.

"Hello, Dan. Hello, Joan," Mike said.

"My name is Jean," she explained, "Jean."

Whamo! Mike could imagine her mind doing those cartwheels again.

Well, let's say Mike had evened the scorecard with Jean or Joan or whatever her name is. Well, at least until the next time he runs into her.

In another example, let me tell you about a farewell party I attended. Ken was leaving after having worked for the company for six years. Ken's boss was a guy named Jim Patterson. Patterson was, by all accounts, a bungler who did very little to inspire, lead, or help his employees.

In his farewell speech, Ken thanked everyone for being so kind and helpful. Especially, he said, he wanted to thank his boss, Jim Peterson, for all of his help and assistance. And then he made a couple of other references to his boss, referring to him as Jim *Peterson* each time.

I watched Patterson's face every time Ken called him Peterson. I imagine he was thinking thoughts, like, "He worked for me six years, and he doesn't even know my name." "I matter that little to him?" "I made no stronger impression than that?" "I wish I'd have fired the S.O.B. before he quit."

I don't know if Ken called Patterson *Peterson* by mistake or on purpose. What I do know is that it cut Patterson-Peterson to the quick.

Well, there are a few examples of some of the biggest ego busters, I've ever seen. In many ways, they're perfect examples of how to get even through finesse. The technique is simple — anyone can use it. It's direct, going straight for the heart. You can get them and they know you've got them. But, they'll never know for sure if you got them on purpose or if it was a pure and simple slip of the tongue or lapse of memory. But, deep-down, they probably know. Perfect.

THE CLOUD OF SMOKE

It's something that had hung over my head like a cloud of smoke for almost forty years.

It started back when I was a kid, about ten years old, and my cousin, Andy, was about eight. Our family went to visit Andy's family one Sunday afternoon. It was fun to visit Andy, because he lived on a farm where there were all sorts of buildings and a big grove to play in. And Aunt Harriet always made lots of great cakes and pies for desert.

Andy and I played a little catch in the yard and then headed for the grove for a little exploring. Andy led me to a spot behind some bushes out of sight of the house. He reached into those bushes and dug around for a little while and finally pulled out a glass jar.

Andy held that glass jar up in front of my eyes and got a big, devilish grin on his face.

"Where'd you get that?" I asked as I stared at the pack of cigarettes and matches in the glass jar.

As Andy screwed open the lid on the jar, he explained that a friend had stolen them from his father's carton and had sold them to Andy.

Andy pulled two cigarettes out of the pack — Lucky Strikes without a filter. He stuck one in his mouth and handed the other to me. This was my first encounter with two experiences that have plagued many a young man — peer pressure and smoking. I really didn't want to smoke, or, more accurately, I suppose, I wanted to but was scared to try it. Well, whatever the reason, I lit up just like Andy.

Andy and I took a few puffs and blew smoke in the air and thought we were pretty grown-up. Neither of us inhaled (hey, we could run for President) but Andy said he thought he knew how to do it. He took a big drag on that Lucky Strike and inhaled the smoke all the way down to his toes. That part worked pretty well, but when Andy tried to exhale the smoke, he must have swallowed or something. He started coughing and sputtering and wheezing something awful. It's the first time I ever saw anyone turn green or ever saw a person's eyes spin in opposite directions.

After about ten minutes of coughing and wheezing and sputtering, and shaking, Andy finally recovered enough to stand with a little help from me. All Andy wanted to do was go in the house and go to bed.

I was afraid that Andy and I would really get into trouble for smoking, but neither my parents nor Andy's suspected a thing. In fact, Aunt Harriet attributed Andy's sudden illness to "that flu bug that has been going around." She lovingly tucked him into bed and even made him some soup to make him feel better.

About a week later, my mother talked to Aunt Harriet on the phone, and she said that Andy had finally confessed that he had been smoking. But it really wasn't his fault, you see, because his older cousin, Peter (that's me, remember) had brought a pack of cigarettes along and had pressured him into smoking against his will. Lucky Strikes without a filter, to boot. Poor Andy. Evil Peter.

Needless to say, I received a severe tongue lashing from my mother, for all sorts of things — smoking, pressuring Andy into smoking, getting Andy sick, lying, and so on.

At this stage, my credibility wasn't too hot, and, no matter how I tried to explain what had really happened, it fell on deaf ears.

Fast-forward about forty years.

Cousin Andy grew up to be one of the finest people I've ever known, and we get along great to this day. Aunt Harriet's still one of the neatest people I know, and she's always treated me just fine. But, still, through the forty years since "the incident," there were times when I could tell by the look in her eyes that she still remembered me as "the sneaky little weasel who got my Andy sick from smoking cigarettes."

About this time, four of my mother's and Aunt Harriet's cousins from France came to the United States for a visit. My mother hosted a noon luncheon for them, and about a dozen of us turned out to greet them, including Andy and me.

It was a great time, telling them all sorts of family stories and listening to theirs. Finally, of course, somebody got around to mentioning something about "two young boys smoking." Everybody in the family knew the story, and someone told the old family tale to the visitors, much to everyone's enjoyment, except, perhaps, for one person.

When the laughter stopped, I said, "Well, that story's almost right."

"What do you mean?" someone asked.

"All except for the part about who had the stuff," I said, looking at cousin Andy with a raised eyebrow.

There was a moment of silence, and then Andy looked straight at his mother and said, "I did."

Well, it almost knocked Aunt Harriet off her chair. And my

mother, too. And the rest of them. For almost forty years I was known as "The weasel who had led little cousin Andy down the evil path to smoking his first cigarette." Now the truth came out. It felt like a big cloud of smoke that had hung over me for all these years had just blown away.

Looking back at it, it wasn't any big deal. Andy and me smoking a cigarette. It wasn't any big deal that the commonly-believed version of the story wasn't quite right, and the whole thing never became a big deal that placed any strain on family relationships.

I will admit, though, I have renewed faith in the old saying, "The truth shall set you free." And I have renewed faith that if you are patient, the truth will come out, eventually, even though it might take forty years or so.

LET'S GET SERIOUS

Yes, let's talk about something serious for a moment — death. That's about as serious as it gets, because, religious views notwithstanding, after death nothing else matters. Or does it?

Death. You die, somebody plans a nice service for you, they have the service, complete with a few organ tunes and a few kind words, six good men carry you from the church to the hearse, the hearse hauls you to the cemetery, everybody gathers around you for a few last words of good-bye, they go back to the church for lunch, and somebody stays behind to put you in your place. They wouldn't stay behind, either, you know, except that they're paid to do it — and with your money, to boot.

And that's the way it usually goes. But every now and then some character gets creative and takes a hand in planning their own funeral and makes plans for themselves for after their funeral. Those are my kind of people — the ones who refuse to die even after they're dead.

Take my friend, Sid, for example. When he dies, he wants to be stuffed and mounted instead of being buried. He wants his wife to sit him in his favorite rocking chair and set it in the corner of the living room. That way, he figures, his family won't have to go through the ordeal and expense of a funeral, and it'll kind of be like he's just sitting there, asleep. They can even talk to him if they get lonesome or if they want to have a nice visit with somebody who won't interrupt or argue. Since Sid is a pretty quiet fellow even now, while he's, supposedly, alive, carrying on a conversation with him after he's stuffed and mounted won't be a whole lot different than talking to him right now, live and in person.

Another crony, Gary, believes in high-tech. He was the first guy I ever knew who could actually run a home computer and he can even program his VCR. Gary believes that someday in the future, maybe 100 years from now, they'll have plastic replacement parts for every part of the human body. When something wears out, you'll simply go to a store, much like a present-day auto parts store, and get the part you need. Some kind of a surgeon, similar to a present-day master mechanic, will put the new part in, tune you up, and you'll be good for another hundred thousand miles. That being the case, Gary wants to be frozen when he dies so that, when the new technology hits, they can thaw him out and overhaul him.

Then, let me tell you about Eddie. Eddie spends every spare moment of his life fishing, and he loves the water. When he dies, he wants to be cremated and wants to have his ashes scattered on the waters of his favorite fishing spot, Lake Okoboji. He kind of visualizes himself gently riding the waves into the sunset, searching for that big one that always got away.

Well, those are all pretty good plans for having one last bit of fun, but each of these plans has a fatal flaw. Sid, for instance, sitting there stuffed and mounted, might make a pretty good conversation piece, and his wife and kids and grandkids might get some comfort from having him around. But three or four generations from now what are they gonna do — use him for a hat rack? They'll never be able to sell him at a garage sale, and it's not the sort of thing you can put out on the curb with the garbage.

And the cost of paying the electrical bill to keep Gary frozen for 100 years will cost approximately two million dollars, considering inflation, and it's doubtful that any shirttail relative down the line will want to foot the bill for that. And besides, if Gary's heirs are anything like Gary, it won't take them long to figure out that the freezer could be put to better use cooling down beer than cooling down Gary.

And even though Eddie visualizes his ashes floating off into the sunset, the truth is that the first time a motorboat comes along, he'll be turned to mud.

But I have my own plan for having a little fun after I'm gone. No, I'm not going to be stuffed and mounted or frozen or cremated. I'm going to go along with the normal program with a normal service, the hearse ride, and all that stuff, ending up six feet under like all the other normal people. But I do want those six good men to parade me around the block a time or two before they put me in the hearse. And I'm gonna leave a couple of thousand dollars in the hands of a trusted friend to throw everybody one last good party — but not the night of the funeral. I want them to mourn me for a minimum of three days, first.

But here's where I'll really have my fun. I'm going to hide notes all over the house for my wife to stumble across for years to come after I'm gone. Hundreds of them. Some will be sweet, like "Even though I'm not with you right now, I still love you, dear," and "You were the one true love of my life."

Other notes will be designed to make sure my wife remembers me and all the good times we had, like, "Remember the time we saw the Righteous Brothers in concert — wasn't that a blast!" or "Next time you eat at The Hollywood Grill, say hello to everybody for me."

Still others will be to tease her, like, "Did you ever figure out how I got that pink lipstick on my shirt collar," or "Didn't you ever think it was strange that I went on hunting trips all those years, and I never owned a gun."

And then, I'm going to leave a few notes around for my wife's new husband. Like maybe I'll put a note in my sock drawer that says, "Boo! Get the hell out of my sock drawer."

I'm going to have so much fun, I can't wait to die.

At least I thought that way until I made the mistake of telling my wife about my plans for after I'm gone. The party idea she liked, but being paraded around the block is out. And she said she'd burn the house down if she found even so much as one note.

That's the problem with some people — they take death too seriously.